Soul-Selfie

#NoFilter

Soul-Selfie
#NoFilter

Heather Carter

Carpenter's Son Publishing

Soul-Selfie #NoFilter

Published by Carpenter's Son Publishing, Franklin, Tennessee

Published in association with Larry Carpenter of
Christian Book Services, LLC
www.christianbookservices.com

Edited by Ann Tatlock

Interior Layout Design by Suzanne Lawing

Cover and Cover Illustration by Emma Carter

Printed in the United States of America

978-1-952025-71-6

This collection of blogs is dedicated to my husband of 30 years, Blake Carter. He was my best friend in high school and is still my favorite person. He knows all the ways I fall short and don't live up to all I "preach," but he accepts me and cherishes me anyway. He is my example of someone who is willing to go to any length to be emotionally and spiritually strong and healthy. He overflows with grace and has a history of preaching the same message of hope and transformation as I do. We make a good team.

Love you, baby.

I also want to dedicate this book to my momma (Peggy Ahlstrom)! It would be absurd to say I miss having leukemia, but she and I both miss the freedom we had to "hang out" both at the hospital and at my house as I recovered. Those were excruciating but also sweet times that we both cherish. My dad (Craig Ahlstrom) was always there to support and sacrifice his time with my mom so she could be with me. I can still hear his voice saying, "If you and your mom are happy, I'm happy."

Grateful for you both.

Contents

Why I Write ...

It's probably fair to say that "let me explain" is not the most stellar introduction for a book. But I feel like I might as well be up front with you and tell you that I am not a "real writer." I am just a girl who started blogging about her leukemia journey and can't seem to stop.

In 2015 I was diagnosed with Acute Myeloid Leukemia (read: "abrupt and devastating interruption to life as you know it"). Due to a secondary infection, I was intubated and in ICU for a week. There were a good number of people who feared I would not wake up but by the grace of God, and some sound medical advice from my husband Blake (no, he is not a doctor ☺), I did. I woke up feisty and have maintained that fighting spirit ever since.

Over a seven-month stretch, I spent 70 days in the hospital. After the first week, Blake started a blog site so we could update people on my status. As I began to recover, but while I was still confined to the hospital room for six days at a time for chemo, my blog became cathartic in getting me outside of my head. I started to share my fears, struggles, inspirations, and spiritual observations with those who read. I told on myself about the raw, messy, embarrassing and often ugly thoughts and feelings I had about what was happening to me and why.

Eventually I was even able to find ways to be grateful for what my disease had triggered in me and in my life. My blog went from updating people on the health and healing of my body to reflections on the health and healing of my soul.

What surprised me was that even though I was often sharing about my own disease and what I was learning from the experience, other people seemed to relate and be encouraged by what I wrote. Like I said, I didn't see myself as a writer (I had never written anything in my previous, pre-cancer life, nor did I want to), so this confused me. But my writing itself was not what was inspiring them. It was the connection they felt to someone who made them feel like they were not alone in their pain, their struggle, their *weirdness*, if you will.

I write a lot about cancer, how I'm affected by others' addictions, and ultimately the universal diseases of the soul. Diseases like worry, fear, control, comparison, and resentment, just to name a few. Apparently, I am not the only one who has these diseases. I used to worry that when my cancer went into remission, my writing would go into remission with it. But since the diseases of the soul, the "common plagues of the heart" as I call them, are chronic, it seems I will never run out of material. I have proven this to be true, since this is now my second book. My first book, *Soul-Selfie*, covers the first 120 blogs I wrote during my leukemia battle. *Soul-Selfie: #NoFilter* covers the aftermath.

Even though I write about a variety of topics, there is one theme that presents itself in every single entry: ME. My soul. I write about what I observe, struggle with, screw up, celebrate and grieve. I talk about what I believe in with all my heart, what I wish I could believe, and what I am completely confounded and confused by. I touch on territory in my soul that I have come to find out also exists in yours.

I love when I hear from someone who identifies with my craziness. Because that's the beauty of it. We are not alone in our hurt, our failures, our passions, and our longing to be better than we are today.

We're not the only ones. What a relief.

When talking with my sister-in-law a few months ago, she said, "It's like God used cancer to root out a cancer in you that has nothing to do with cancer." Ooohhh, that's good (she's much deeper and more well-spoken than me). Yep. God has gone to town on my soul. And unfortunately, or fortunately, I think He's got His work cut out for Him! I don't see any end in sight, but I do see progress. And honestly, that's probably the most one can hope for in this life.

So, why *Soul-Selfie: #NoFilter*? Because I have wasted way too much time looking outward. Taking pictures of other people's behavior and either judging it or trying to imitate it. Cancer and writing have been my cues to tap on that little icon on my "I"-phone camera and flip the focus back on myself.

Instead of focusing on you, I have to look at me. But as I take my Soul-Selfies and share them with you, maybe we can be broken and vulnerable together. We can remind ourselves that there is always hope and we are all in this together.

Why they read...

It's hard to answer when someone asks me who my "target audience" is. Basically, if you have a soul, you are my target audience. See below to hear from readers from all walks of life and age ranges…

Heather writes *from* the heart, straight *to* the heart. The reason her words are powerful is that we know she's walked the same road we are traveling. And through her experience, she can speak hope and healing into our souls.

—BRETT DETKEN, Professor at University of Nevada Las Vegas

If you could see the books on my nightstand, *Soul-Selfie* sits on top. Heather's message resonates across a wide spectrum of experiences and emotions, thus the need for the ready proximity at the top of the pile. My personal relationship with Heather extends almost 20 years, but that's an extra blessing of knowing the consistent nature of her character. If we'd never met, my prayer would be she started writing sooner so more people would have the advantage of her spirit-filled love of others and life in general.

—BILL SCHOMBERG, Corporate Strategist

Soul-Selfie: #NoFilter is so downright human that it seems to be a book that any of us could have written ... IF, that is, we were all as gifted as Heather Carter to be able to probe deeply, pursue the truth uncompromisingly, and visualize poetically the events and emotions that make each of our lives an epic of their own.

—Robert Lackie, Seminary Student

Heather was an exuberant student of mine at Ozark Christian College. In the many years since she was a college girl, she has had both wonderful and difficult experiences. It has been a kind of joy to watch her embrace the good and bad in life and give every bit of it over to God. Life is joy and sorrow, and Heather's struggle to let Him lead through both is familiar to any who desire to be fully His. These pages are full of her journey with so many implications for ours.

—Jackina Stark, Author of *Tender Grace* and retired English Professor at Ozark Christian College

I heard about *Soul-Selfie* from a mutual friend.This book is amazing. It has helped me reunite with people from my past. It has given me closure on some issues that needed to be closed. It's a book that I looked forward to reading every day. It's a book I will definitely read again.

—Brian Bera, Corporate Pilot

How to read ...

Once you start reading, it won't take long for you to recognize one of my signature character defects: control. So, we might as well kick off our journey together with me giving you some "gentle-bossy advice" on how I would want you to read my book.

Although I would love for you to throw this book in your suitcase for a good read on the beach, it's not designed for that. Even though I hope and pray my book does not bore you, its intent is not for entertainment. It's meant for comfort and challenge and change.

My hope is that you will read one or two blog posts a day and reflect on the message of it. I never ever write for "fun." My brain doesn't work like that. I mentioned earlier that I am not a "real writer." I only write when I am enlightened or in some sort of discontent or turmoil. I typically write about what is happening deep in my soul—ugliness and all. I write to "reason it out" on paper so I don't go completely crazy holding it in. By the time I finish approximately 750 words, God gives me answers that would have come to me in no other way.

I encourage you to put this book somewhere that you will read it and refer to it regularly. And for the love of Pete, underline and write in it! When you finish it, start over and notice how you have grown or maybe slipped. This time, use a different pen or highlighter, because what I have found is that, depending on your current circumstances, certain entries will jump off the page that didn't affect you at all the first time through.

For me, taking a soul-selfie is about as painful as taking a real selfie. In my experience, neither is pleasant. However, if you lean in, maybe this book will help you embrace your experiences and use them to find hope and share it with others. If it helps, when reading, try to ask yourself these same four questions for every entry:

1. How have I experienced/thought/felt something similar in my life?
2. If it is past tense, how has my attitude/belief/thinking changed as a result?
3. If it is a present situation/thought/belief pattern, what can I do to gain perspective/hope/healing/celebration in it?
4. Who do I know that might benefit from reading this?

Though I would be thrilled for you to share *Soul-Selfie: #NoFilter* with others, this is not a book you pass on to someone else. They will need a clean copy so they can underline what stands out to them. If they can't afford a copy, buy one for them or email me at heathercartersoulselfie@gmail.com and I will personally mail one to them.

As you move along in the readings, you may observe that my solutions often morph depending on where I am in my life journey. Don't freak out. This is not a "how to" book. It's a book about who, how and what it takes to help me stay sane and serene. That means my solution by blog 342 might differ from the solution that worked for me in blog 25. People grow and change, so don't call me out if I contradict myself. The trials of life bring about many new perspectives, especially over the three-year period in which these blogs were written.

So, enough instruction on how to read. I pray that you will feel that I am right there with you in whatever you may be going through. Even if it's just you and me, my desire is that you will know in your spirit that you are not alone. We can do this together.

*This is a non-staged picture of my friend Bill's nightstand. He sent this to me when I asked him if he would be willing to write a testimonial about why he reads my blogs. This is a picture of the first edition: *Soul-Selfie*. I hope your nightstand will look the same.

**Disclaimer: all emojis have been preserved from original blogs* ☺

"Trigger-happy"

Does anyone else have "triggers"? I remember a superficial trigger I used to have when I was pregnant with my oldest child. Before that time, I was an exercise and health-food Nazi. In college, while all the girls were ordering pizza at 10:00 at night, I was eating my SnackWell's Cookies (which may or may not have contributed to other health problems ... who knows what's in those!) and heading off to sleep. So, when I got pregnant, I went crazy. I ate whatever I wanted whenever I wanted it. It was heavenly. One day, when I had determined that I would eat like a responsible adult, I was at a stoplight and caught a whiff of the most glorious aroma--Burger King. I could smell the burgers grilling from inside my car with the windows up. I have never liked Burger King burgers because I prefer the fried greasy burgers at McDonalds. But not when I was pregnant, apparently. I circled back and got in that drive-through. I ate the best-testing flame-broiled burger ever. I eventually had to start taking an alternate route to the store so the smell of the grill didn't trigger a relapse of cheeseburger scarfing.

Luckily, now that I am not pregnant, I can drive smugly past any Burger King without giving it another glance--or sniff. Unfortunately, I have allowed some more serious triggers to invade my life. A trigger is anything that diverts me from where I am intending to go and gets me all turned around sideways and lost in a bad part of my mind where it is not safe to go alone. Sometimes I know these triggers are coming and sometimes they blindside me. When I know they are coming, I do my best to be prepared by asking God to be with me and go ahead of me and also to stand between me and the trigger at hand.

A few years ago, things got kind of rocky in my world. I lost many relationships and others were strained and fragile. During that season, I went back to work full time. On my daily commute, I had to (I guess I *chose* to) pass several homes/cars/locations that would trigger painful memories of what had been lost. By the time I got to work, even if I had prepared, I was often a mess of angst and grief. *All* this before I even walked in the doors to start my workday.

I used to wish I could just move out of this town so my emotions weren't on high alert everywhere I went. Like I said, I suppose I could have chosen to go a different way to work, but for the same reason I didn't move away, I decided that I wanted to deal with my pain, not avoid it. Besides, wherever you go, there you are. I would take this pain with me one way or another. By driving past all these places from my "past," I was forced to deal or die. If I didn't ask God for help and peace and the ability to own my part and to forgive, my daily commute to work would generate bitterness and resentment that would prevent me from loving and receiving love. It was one of the hardest lessons I ever had to learn. A long one, too.

I still have triggers. This morning I was reading from *Jesus Calling* and it reminded me that God is saying, "When you start to feel stressed, let those feelings alert you to your need for Me. Thus, your needs become doorways to deep dependence on Me and increasing intimacy between us."[1] When I read that, I made up my mind to focus on that today. To turn to Him in utter dependence whenever thoughts or circumstances or people trigger stress in my heart. And isn't it just like God to give me ample and prompt opportunity to prove it! The first time wasn't even a trigger; it felt more like a full-fledged firing squad! My heart raced, anxiety through the roof ... and then I sensed Him gently reminding me to use this as an opportunity to look to Him. To ask Him for serenity in my spirit. To extend forgiveness and compassion to another person who also is walking this road of life and has hit a few bumps of their own.

And, as luck (or God) would have it, as I am writing He gave me yet *another* trigger (bless His heart ...) to remind me where my identity and peace come from.

So ask yourself ... what are your triggers and what kinds of behaviors do they trigger? I am pretty convinced that the triggers themselves will never go away. But maybe instead of responding to them with actions or thoughts that are harmful to me and those around me, I can use them to trigger my sheer, desperate dependence on God alone to steady, soothe, and still my heart and mind. Instead of dreading the "triggers" I can become "trigger-happy."

Interference!

Does anyone else seem to have to learn lessons the hard way? Good grief ...

So, here's how it went down: yesterday morning I had a fantastic idea for a blog rolling around in my head. For some reason the word "interfere" came to my mind during, um, church (sorry, God). As I thought about this word, I realized that if I were dictating the word "interfere" to my phone, it might be translated into text as "inner fear." Sounds the same when spoken. And so of course, thinking about words and their meanings caused me to look up the definition of "interfere." Here it is: "to take part or intervene in an activity without invitation or necessity." Some synonyms are "to barge into, pry into, intrude into, get involved in, encroach on, impinge on." None of them sounds very positive, if you ask me. It occurred to me the times I have interfered in someone's life or business, the reason has primarily been my own "inner fear." Fear of not getting what I want or someone not doing what I want or losing something I already have or think I have control over.

Fast forward to when I returned home from church about an hour later ... I walked right into my house and did exactly that to my poor, unsuspecting husband. I accused and assumed and "intervened without invitation or necessity." It was awful. Even as the words were flowing out of my mouth, I was already regretting them (anyone relate?). I felt physically sick over my reaction to my own "inner fear" that drove me to "interfere." How often have I done this to people? Sometimes I can tell myself that I am doing it for their own good. But, in actuality, I am giving advice and direction and "help" to people who haven't asked for it. This is not loving. It is self-serving. It's an attempt to alleviate my own sense of feeling powerless. I want to have some control. I want others to do what I think is best for them. When I interfere, I get in the way of what God is trying to do in them.

In Recovery, we talk a lot about "hitting bottom." Getting to the place where you are so low, the only direction you can possibly go is up. When we interfere out of our own "inner fear," we interrupt that process and possibly distract and deter those around us from what God is trying to do in them. Interference is an attempt to make ourselves feel better, to squelch our anxiety over another person's actions or lifestyle. It is not loving, as we often claim as our honorable excuse, to butt in where we don't belong.

I tend to have to learn things the hard way. Please God, let this experience be a turning point for me. I am tired of having to "re-learn" it (and so is my husband, probably ☺).

I wanna be a hosta!

It's hotter than Hades here in Illinois. So, naturally, we picked this week to plant grass seed and new shrubs (which I purchased at the bargain price of "buy it now for practically nothing because it could potentially die on your drive home"). I took approximately three showers yesterday just from doing regular life stuff. I knew that my plants were in grave danger if I didn't give them a good shower themselves. So here is what I am dealing with: I planted a few new shrubs (on their death-bed before they even hit the dirt) and some herbs, spread the grass seed and transplanted some bushes from one part of my yard to another. All of this requires a rigorous, daily watering regimen. If I don't spend about 20 minutes watering these new seeds/plants, they will surely wither and scorch in the heat. I do not have a green thumb so their life expectancy is still to be determined.

Here's what I was thinking as I stood, sweating profusely, watering my new plants yesterday: "I may have made an enormous mistake. I should have stuck to hostas and called it a day." Are you familiar with hostas? My front yard is full of them. I love hostas because: one, I am cheap and you can split these and replant portions of them other places without having to spend money, and two, you have to work really hard to kill them. Even when you split them you can just hack off a few leaves with teeny tiny roots at the end and literally shove them in some dirt and they will live. Once you plant them, you can throw a little bit of water their way initially, then leave them alone and they will grow with very little attention. That's my kind of landscaping: Plant. Water. Ignore. Enjoy.

I wish I were a hosta kind of girl. I wish I could read, meditate, or pray occasionally and attend a weekly church service or Recovery meeting and continue to grow at a lovely, flourishing pace. But alas-I am more of a newly transplanted shrub that has been planted in scalding hot temperatures and harsh conditions. If I don't "water" regularly I will surely wilt and eventually die. The reality for me is that inspiration and motivation leak. I can read a phenomenal passage in the morning or spend quiet time meditating, and by the time I finish breakfast I have lost my serenity and am off and running with worry and fear leading the way.

I don't know the "why" of it, but God did not design us to live like hostas. He wants us to depend on Him for the refreshment and nourishment that come when we look to Him on a consistent basis. I used to think that meant every morning I should rise and start my day with Him. I still believe that gets me off to a good start, but it's only a start. Unless I turn to Him for guidance and strength to make every decision, to respond lovingly to every person, to see the world beyond my selfish plans, I start to shrivel under the harsh conditions of the world. The heat gets to me. My beauty begins to fade. My life expectancy is questionable.

A song that I have on a CD in my car and turn to regularly (song number 14 ...) reminds me of what I need to pray in order to survive the Heat of the Day: All day. Everyday.

"I need You; Oh, I need You. **Every hour (Read: every second of every minute) I need You.** My one defense, my righteousness, Oh God, how I need You."[2]

"Off the wagon"

It's already 4:00 in the afternoon. As a general rule, I am fresher and more motivated to write in the mornings. But not today. Last night I "fell off the wagon." Anyone else have a wagon? They are very bumpy and susceptible to potholes and inclement road conditions. You really do have to be paying pretty close attention to ride on it without incident. There are lots of different types of wagons to fall from, and last night mine was the "Emotional Sobriety" wagon. I didn't break anything, but I have many lingering injuries. I had been riding said wagon at a pretty consistent clip for a good stretch of time. I was actually fairly proud of this. In hindsight, the best kind of sight there is, I may have been a little cocky, which led to carelessness, which led to me falling backwards off the wagon. I have fallen off some other wagons before. The "Healthy Eating" wagon is always a crowded and popular one. A close second is probably the "Daily Exercise" wagon. Then there are the more intense wagon rides whose passengers are holding on for dear life most of the time: the "Addiction" wagons.

So, how did I end up on my backside on the ground as my Emotional Sobriety wagon carried on without me? The specifics aren't important, but I will say that I basically got so wound up, so angry, so fearful, and so overwhelmed with the powerlessness I have over other people's choices, that I completely failed to utilize all the "tools" I have studied and read about and prayed for to help me ride safely ON the wagon. Tools like "Live and let live," and "Let Go and Let God," and "Pause, Pray and Proceed." I ignored my resolve to practice not interfering with others' decisions or trying to get others to do what I think will bring them happiness. I forgot to do MY job and tried to do GOD'S job--the biggest mistake of all. So in all my scurrying around trying to do the opposite of what keeps me "Emotionally Sober," I fell off. Hard.

I woke up groggy and with an "Emotional Hangover." So disappointed in myself. I had hurt people I love, including me. I had acted as if I had no solution to my fears and worries and insanity. Part of me wanted to just crawl back into bed and give up. Thoughts like, "I'm an idiot. I stink. I'm a failure. I'll never be able to be the mature woman I want to be. I quit." The temptation was to just accept that I am a loser and start walking along the bumpy road; who needs that stupid wagon anyway?!

And yet, God graciously, mercifully, showed me another solution. I could get back on. Could it be that simple? Think about it, people ... It's a WAGON. It's not a Ferrari that sped away and left me abandoned on the highway. Wagons are slow. Chances are, even with my injuries, I could still catch it and hop back on. The fall doesn't have to be FATAL. I could get on and keep riding. Only now, I am smarter and wiser about how I ride. I am more cautious when I see a bumpy road approaching. I hold on. I pray. I get my tools ready to use. You can do this too. So you ate a sleeve of Chips Ahoy last night? ... Tonight you can have some fruit. Drank a few too many beers or broke a streak of abstinence? ... Crawl back on the wagon and keep going. Spent a week/month/year neglecting your conscious contact with God? ... Get your "Spiritual" wagon out of that-there barn, dust if off and get moving! It's never ever too late to hop, or crawl, back onto that wagon.

"Your mercies are new every morning; great is your faithfulness, O God." Lamentations 3:23

Overqualified

I considered titling this entry "I'm Still Sick." Then I reconsidered. Didn't want anyone to panic. No, I don't still have leukemia, at least that I'm aware of. But hang with me for a couple minutes and I'll explain ...

My two youngest kids were visiting grandparents on the west coast for the past few weeks. My husband and I and our college-age son were "home alone." With all my free time, I made big plans to write and read and redecorate and sell lots of houses. I did a few of those things, but the one I didn't do, at all, was write. I had plenty of time. That excuse wouldn't work. In fact, I went so long without a blog entry that I considered the possibility that maybe my writing days were over. I told myself I had nothing worthwhile to say. I was experiencing doubts and distractions and discouragement in almost every area of life that mattered to me. What could I possibly share that wouldn't be hypocritical? So I just stopped writing. *I wasn't qualified.*

But then, God gently reminded me that I started writing these blogs when I was sick with leukemia.

I was qualified to share my heart and perspective on how it was affecting me and those around me. And this is the part where I remind myself that I am still "sick." Whether I am sick with a physical disease or a spiritual disease, it all counts. Life is hard. It can be painful. It can even be so emotionally draining that one longs for leukemia again just to distract from the suffering. Now *that's* messed up!

Maybe that's my point--this blog started when I was pretty messed up. The good and bad news is that I am still messed up. I write because it helps me remember that depending on God for my serenity and sanity is a minute-by-minute activity. I am sick with some pretty ugly character defects and sinful tendencies, and, unlike leukemia, I will never be declared "cured" in this lifetime. But because of God's grace, I know I have been made clean in His eyes. How I look in other people's eyes is different, though. My hope is that you can read what I say and feel the assurance that maybe you're not alone on this ride. Maybe together we can lift each other up and cheer each other on and tend to each other's wounds. If the reason I write is to share my mistakes and failures and doubts and flaws so that together we can manage this life with compassion and acceptance and without judgment, then guess what? I will never run out of material. *I think I am more than qualified.*

Seekest thou great things for thyself?

10:00 a.m. … I might as well just tell you up front ... I am afraid this entry will be filled with mostly questions that I am not sure I can answer in one sitting. Actually, I am not sure I can ever answer them solidly. But maybe you have some better ideas than I do. Or maybe you have had some similar questions but have been unwilling to admit them to anyone or yourself, for that matter. So, let's get on with it ...

I read something a few days ago that has been haunting me. Mostly because it raises a really good point, but I was left without a practical, real-life solution to remedy the question the author, Oswald Chambers, posed (using Jeremiah 14:5 "seekest thou great things for thyself?"). He asked, "Are you seeking great things from God for yourself? God wants you in a closer relationship to Himself than receiving His gifts, He wants you to get to know HIM ... there is nothing easier than getting into a right relationship with God except when it is not God Whom you want but only what He gives."[3] Ouch.

Basically, when God is viewed that way, our love for Him is conditional, dependent on what He does or has done for us. Or what He has or hasn't allowed to happen in our lives. That is childish (not to be confused with "child-like"). Think about it in human relationships. Do you feel valuable, cherished, loved for who you are, if the only time your spouse or parents or children engage with you is when you give them something they want or are reminded of something you have already done for them? Gratitude is important. And I believe we should always be thanking God for His good gifts, but I am struggling to think of how to connect with Him just because I love Him. When you can't go to coffee or a movie or hear a band on a Saturday night, how do I "get to know Him" without reviewing what He has done for me in the past or asking Him to please do something on my "list" right now?

1:30 p.m. ... So, for the first time ever in my blog writing, I took a break and am finishing this up hours after I started. I needed to get away from home and think about this, so I went and worked out. I am not sure if the thoughts that came to me will help you, but they did help me to at least make a beginning of it (feel free to weigh in with your own ideas). On a side note, I about killed myself trying to type my ideas into my notes on my phone while on the elliptical machine at the Y.

Here are some obvious thoughts that have probably already occurred to you but were helpful to me in sorting out my questions:

1) When my kids were little, they really didn't care too much about "connecting" with me. They

ultimately wanted to feel safe, be well-fed and sufficiently housed (which equals warm and stocked with toys). Most of why they felt love for me was a result of what I DID for them. As they have grown, that is beginning to change. Especially for my college student. He calls occasionally, but over the past two years it has become more about "checking in" about life and less about sending him money or stuff. Why is that? Because he is maturing. Growing up. As I mature and "grow up" in my relationship with God, I start trusting Him not just because of what He does for me (even though, as with my own kids, we have a history of being cared for and receiving gifts) but because I love and trust Him. That's how mature minds think. How mature relationships work. People, and God, don't have to do stuff for us or give things to us in order for us to love them. Now, that makes sense to me.

2) Which leads me to this idea of faith. I learn to have faith in God, to trust and love Him even when I don't get the answer I want. I love the example of Job (that dude from the Bible that had every possible tragedy fall upon him), who tells his friends (the same friends who told him to "curse God and die" already) that he believed God would help him. But then he adds, "but

EVEN IF HE DOES NOT ..." I will still praise Him. When I trust God with the unknown, I show my love for Him is not conditional on me getting my way.

3) Lastly, at least as far as this entry is concerned, it hit me that there can be no love without SERVING. I can learn to love God selflessly when I ask Him to make me into the type of person (kind, compassionate, patient, tolerant, etc.) who demonstrates to others that I love Him and that I love them. Asking for those types of things isn't for me, they are to help me live out God's greatest commandments ... love God and love people. When I serve others and serve God (through my obedience to His ways), I give evidence that the relationship is not one-sided. It's not about me getting or keeping what I want. Don't get me wrong, asking Him in faith to answer all kinds of prayers is fabulous. Keep it up! I kicked leukemia in the butt because many of you did just that! But try to push yourself farther. Try to focus on growing up in your relationship with God. Loving Him in an unconditional, mature way.

I want to regularly ask myself if it is God that I want, or do I just want something from Him?

Live and let live

Today I am writing as a result of what I like to affectionately call a "Divine Accident." Translated, this refers to an instance where I do something without accessing all my brain connectors and end up landing on a truth or lesson that I would have missed otherwise. God knows who He's dealing with. My sister and I further describe this common family trait by saying there's no "ZZZT" between the two sides of our brain. So, I was reading a great entry in a book this morning, and it gave me a scripture to look up. I thought it was Psalm 118:17. This is what it said: "I will not die, but live, and will proclaim what the Lord has done." Well. That is certainly blunt. It actually made me laugh. Then I realized that I was reading the wrong verse. I was supposed to be looking up Psalm 18:17.

I'm not blaming God for my spacey-ness, but I still believe that He wanted me to read that particular verse. If you have ever met me in person, you may or may not have noticed that I often operate in the "extremes" world. My husband affectionately points out quite frequently that I am either freezing or burning up, starving or so full I might never eat again, completely overwhelmed with activity or bored to death; you get the picture. So, when I read a verse that says, "I will not die, but live," I smirk, because I know it's for me to hear in my own "extremes" language.

I am reminded of a slogan from Recovery that says, "Live and Let Live." Most of the time I focus on the "let live" part of that phrase. But when I read a scripture like the one above (I will not die, but LIVE) I am struck by how poorly I have been doing this recently. OK, and even not so recently. It's so easy to get caught up in how other people are behaving or misbehaving or just plain not acting like I want them to, resulting in a life not fully lived.

The reality is that no one will ever live exactly how I wish they would so that I can feel better about my own life. Sometimes people are just not doing it the way we think they should, but there are also many times that people around me do things that are truly harmful or hurtful and give me some pretty good reasons why I should be distressed about my life. But here's the harsh truth of it according to Henry Ward Beecher: "God asks no man whether he will accept life. That is not the choice. You must take it. The only choice is HOW."[4] I have no choice as to how others choose to live. But I do have a choice, and a responsibility, and the privilege of really living my life the way God would have me live it.

It's OK to have joy when those around you are angry. It's OK to smile and be kind to others, even when the circumstances of your life feel precarious, and you are afraid for the future. Not only is it OK, it's the exact remedy for LIVING even when you feel the strongest temptation to postpone the abundant life God offers. Other people? ... They may or may not get better, happier or free-er. Many of us (OK … by us, I mean me) have been "distracted or consumed by the problems of others, and have neglected our own bodies, minds, and spirits."[5] But "Live and Let Live", that simple phrase that is easy enough to remember throughout my day, reminds me that "making a life for ourselves, regardless of what others are doing or not doing, must be a top priority. We have a right to really LIVE, and indeed it is our responsibility to do so."[6]

I WILL NOT DIE, BUT LIVE. PSALM 118:17

A new "bad word"

In the past couple of years I have added a word to my "bad word" list. My list of "bad words" is pretty long because, much to my kid's dismay, I have words on there like "fart" and "butt." I prefer them to use words like "toot" and "bum" like they did when they were three. They are 15, 16 and 20. They may end up getting their "bum" kicked if they use that word at a public high school. But here's my new "bad word" ... FIGURE. Nasty, right? Ya know, when you look it up in the dictionary (or ask Siri to google it) you find that there are about four definitions that use it as a noun and four as a verb. It's apparently a very versatile word. One of the most common ways to use it as a noun is to describe a "figure" as a number in a math problem or in describing a woman's body. Even though I see the logic in this--because quite often I think of my "figure" as a problem to be solved--this is not the "figure" I want to talk about. I am more interested in the verb version.

One of the verb versions of this word means "to calculate or work out"(Merriam-Webster Dictionary). Sometimes I find myself trying to "figure" things out. To calculate them. I am trying to put a figure on something or "crunch the numbers." The thing is, my life is not a math problem that has a definitive answer. I am not a math girl, but I know enough to know that the answer to an equation is either right or it is wrong. No gray area there. Trying to "figure" out life by calculation doesn't work. And to be honest, it gets even worse when I try to use the other definition: "to think, consider, or expect to be the case. To suppose, believe, expect, suspect, conclude, etc." In other words, when I try to use all my power and reasoning skills and take into consideration all that has happened in the past in order to predict the future, I get myself in trouble. I basically try to do God's job and forget that my only job is to move ahead in trust and confidence that He knows what's best for everyone involved and He "sees" what's ahead of me. I don't have to "figure" it out. Because honestly, it's impossible. I am figuring using my limited knowledge and with self-serving ideas leading the way. I want what I want--not always what I need.

So, this is why I have tried to redirect my thinking when I catch myself saying, "I just need to figure it out." I have been doing that a lot lately--trying to figure things out. I have some sort of dilemma and I let it roll around in my head (that's a nice way of confessing that I have been fretting and worrying), trying come up with solutions as to what to do and how it will all work out in the end. Just when I think I have come to the right conclusion, these darn people get involved and then my answers change because I am an emotional being, not a math problem. Here's the thing--the reality is that I can't control other people, places, or things.

All I can really do is turn it over to God and ask him to lead me in the right direction. I don't need to have it all laid out perfectly and then start walking--I just need to point myself in the direction of the next right thing with God at my side and trust Him to lead me to the answer. It sounds childish and simple. I suppose it is. But it is much more effective and less stressful than trying to "figure" it all out. However, since my tendency is to attempt to calculate and figure things out, I need an alternative plan. Instead of using my own calculator, I am determined to only calculate with God in view. "The one thing that keeps us from the possibility of worrying is bringing God in as the greatest factor in all our calculations ."[7] When I can do that, I can truly let it go. Whatever "it" is. It changes minute by minute. I can decide to be overwhelmed with the responsibility of figuring everything out, or I can let my soul rest in the promise of 1 Peter 5:7 ...

"Let God have all your worries and cares, for he is always thinking about you and watching everything that concerns you."

I don't have to "figure it out." That's *God's* job. My job is to trust that He "could and would if he were sought."[8]

"Ism"

I have often heard alcoholism described as a "disease that wants to get you alone and kill you." The emphasis is not on the object of alcohol but on the part about being alone. Isolation. If someone battling this disease tries to fight it on their own--with no support system or program group or sponsor--it will most likely kill them. And without God, it most *definitely* will. I may not struggle with alcohol, but I definitely have tendencies toward the "ism." One definition of "ism" is a "pathological condition." In other words, added to just about anything, "ism" indicates that one's behavior or thought pattern is more harmful than helpful.

Lately I have felt a bit of a combination problem going on. A double-whammy. Some version of "isolation-ism." I'm not exactly laid up in bed, morose and reclusive, but I can identify it mostly by how often I write and if I make efforts to do things with friends I care about. It recently occurred to me that I haven't done either of those things for a very long time. And slowly but surely, if it's not remedied, it will kill my soul. Can anyone relate?

Are you busy but not connected in a real way with anyone? Sitting next to people you know, even family members, feeling painfully alone? Scanning through Facebook getting angry at all those happy people doing fun things? Wishing you had a different life? Feeling like God is on vacation from you specifically? Maybe not. But I have felt this way lately and I really don't like it. It's not the Heather I want to be. The girl who loves her life. Who LIVED through leukemia, for Pete's sake. I certainly did not come back from the dead to live like this. I have a wise mentor who kindly suggested I imagine myself as the Heather I want to be and when the other Heather rears her self-pitying head and complains about the hand she has been dealt, I should politely tell her, "Thanks for sharing. Now sit down and shut up."

One basic recovery principle that I almost forgot that I believed is, "Don't compare your insides with other people's outsides." Just because everything appears perfect or perky in other people's lives, doesn't mean that is their reality. I think the reason for my "isolation-ism" is that I just don't think anyone wants or needs to know that my life is not perfect. That even though God and I conquered cancer, sometimes I feel lonely and useless and defeated.

Wow--are we all sort of scared of/for me right now? I am OK with you feeling that way. Because I suspect some of you might have some of the same crazy thoughts and feelings on any given day. And that's OK too. But we can't let it beat us. This "ism." Your "ism" (defined by Merriam-Webster Dictionary as a "state or condition resulting from an excess of something specific"). When you live with an "ism" at the end of whatever behavior you might be doing to not feel those feelings, to keep up with the Joneses, to try to forget, just for a little while, the fears you have for a loved one's behaviors or your kids' futures--it turns it into a disease. It makes your life a battle of survival. It's exhausting.

Fight hard for the victory and LIVE IN IT. Call a friend. Go on a "date" with someone you love. Cry out to God. Do it again and again and again until you hear from Him. Wait patiently but with expectancy for the mercies He will bring in the morning. He cares for your soul. And remember that at this very moment, whether it's how you want it to be or whether you wish it were different, everything is exactly as it should be and you can trust Him with whatever may come tomorrow.

When I re-read this, it all sounds like a manic rant. I am hesitant to post it, but that is all about my ego. It means my spirit feels extremely vulnerable. It means that someone else might need to "talk about" it too. It means I'll refrain from apologizing if you feel you just wasted the last three minutes of your life. When I write, and share with you some of my craziness, I live out a prayer I pray almost every day. Part of it says:

"God ... take away my difficulties that VICTORY over them may bear witness to those I help of YOUR power, YOUR love, and YOUR way of life. MAY I DO YOUR WILL ALWAYS. Amen."[9]

If sharing my crazy helps you get less crazy ... so be it. ☺

I Want a FastPass

My family loves Disney. Disney anything, really. My husband grew up in LA and therefore had many birthdays and summer/winter/spring jaunts to Disneyland. He has instilled this affection for Disney into our children. We try to go there every other year. We have Disney credit cards (mine has Tinkerbell on it and Blake's has the original black-and-white Mickey). We accumulate points over two years and spend them to buy tickets for four Disney parks at Disney World (in lieu of getting a second mortgage on our house!). We have done this trip enough times with grandparents that we had it down to a science. For years, it involved sending Grandpa to one ride to "get a spot in line and defend it at all costs" until the other six of us arrived.

It worked out well until the invention of the FastPass. Are you familiar? We had to form a new strategy but never fear, we soon had that down to a science as well. We hardly ever had to wait more than 20 minutes in a line. Less astute Disney-park-savvy tourists would glare at us as we skipped past them while they crawled along the winding two-hour trek, sweating and arguing with their children.

Two things changed for us this year: one, we didn't get to bring any grandparents on our trip (I am sitting on my Marriot resort balcony in Orlando as I type--sweating like a fiend, I might add), and two, they came up with yet another "FastPass" system. Apparently, now you have to start planning what rides you want to go on and at what time about a month before you even go on vacation. This is no good for people like me who can't even think about vacation until I am on it.

Here's how it works now: you can schedule three FastPasses at a time. Once you have used them all you can try to schedule another. Once you use that one, if you are lucky enough to find an open slot for five whole people, you can schedule another. I am still deciding if this is brilliant or idiotic on Disney's part. I'll let you know when I finish the Magic Kingdom today.

But ... alas ... I have a point that might actually interest you. I decided that I would really like to have access to some "FastPasses" in my life (I am pretty sure my three were used up years ago). I know which "ride" I want to experience, but the regular line is just too dang long. Not only is it long, it's deceiving. Just when I think I am almost to the end, it does another switchback, and I am right back where I started.

Occasionally, there are respites along the way--like a cool mist, some fans, maybe even an area that has air-conditioning or robotic people/creatures to distract me from the fact that I have been waiting in line for an hour for a 27-second ride. Sometimes things go wrong on the ride ahead and there are delays. It's a very bad sign when you see people sitting in a line that should be moving. They are going absolutely nowhere--they are stuck. And here's what I hate the most about regular lines--watching other people happily jog past me to the very same ride I am slowly trudging toward. It makes the waiting feel even longer and hotter and makes me question whether I even care this much about going on the ride that sounded exciting about 45 minutes ago.

"How long, O Lord?" Have you ever raised your hands to God, or maybe even your tiny fist, and asked Him why it is taking so long to get to the end of the line? How long do I have to suffer this addiction? How long will my kid be bullied? How long until I find my soulmate? How long will it take to live life after losing a parent or spouse or child? How long will it take me to beat this signature sin? How long will I wake up wishing I didn't have to do it one more painful day? How long will my body suffer this disease? How long can I live without a job? How long will you ignore my cries for help? I want change. I want forward movement. I want relief and I want it NOW. I want to be on the ride already. I want a "FastPass."

And yet ... I know that God's timing is always perfect. I can only see right in front of me or a few feet ahead. God sees looking at the whole picture. He is there at the beginning of the line, He is there to lean on while I wait in line, and He knows and sees when I will arrive at the beautiful end of it. I always want to get there faster, but I have to trust that what happens in the line matters as much as what happens when I get to the end of it. How I wait matters. I can be uptight and grouchy and anxious, or I can relax in His presence and let Him carry my heavy backpack filled with worries and fears and dreams that I have tried to force Him to fulfill. I have to wait and TRUST that He knows what I need better than I do. And He knows me inside and out, well enough to know exactly how long it will take.

How Long, O Lord?

Psalm 13

1 How long, O Lord? Will you forget me forever?
How long will you hide your face from me?
2 How long must I take counsel in my soul
and have sorrow in my heart all the day?
How long shall my enemy be exalted over me?
3 Consider and answer me, O Lord my God;
light up my eyes, lest I sleep the sleep of death,
4 lest my enemy say, "I have prevailed over him,"
lest my foes rejoice because I am shaken.
5 But I have trusted in your steadfast love;
my heart shall rejoice in your salvation.
6 ***I will sing to the Lord,***
because he has dealt bountifully with me.

FastPass ... be careful what you wish for!

So ... after I wrote about wanting a "FastPass" a couple days ago (stop reading right now and refer to the previous section if you haven't read it yet ☺), I couldn't help but contemplate what exactly that would look like if it actually could happen in real life. And after a couple days it came to me as subtly as a meteorite landing on my house ... "I have had a FastPass; it was called leukemia." A FastPass gets you through the line, helps you reach your final destination quickly, without distraction, without rest, and with extreme intensity. Yup--that pretty much describes it. There is no sitting down because the line is long and slow and boring. Sometimes you can barely keep up, actually. Whether you want to or not, you have to "just keep walking" toward the end of the line. As you move, you might actually glance at the regular line and wish you could just stop and rest there for a couple minutes--catch your breath. But once you are in the FastPass line, this is not an option any longer.

The thing about real-life FastPasses is that we wish for them in general, but when they actually come, they aren't the kind we've requested. I am sure you have had a few yourself. And as much as they hurt and, to be truthful, feel excruciatingly long for something called a *Fast*Pass, they expedite the rate at which we grow. I sincerely hate to admit this out loud, but it's something we all recognize; we become the kind of person we truly want to be as a result of these FastPass experiences. When we are in situations that require us to keep our connection with God active, when prayer is how we make it through each minute of the day, when we depend on the generosity of others for our health and well-being in a way we never could when we were in the regular line, we get stronger. When we search God's Word for answers and hope and peace because otherwise we would melt into puddles of despair and grief and depression, we get wiser. When we cry out to God and cast every fear, anxiety, and worry at His feet because they are too heavy and burdensome for our weak bodies to carry one more step, we become more of the kind of person others respect and revere and are inspired by. We OVERCOME.

Now that I look back, I know that leukemia has not been the only FastPass I have had the "privilege" to experience. And I know it will not be my final. I think I will prepare myself now for those times ahead. I can do that by keeping my will in line with God's heart. I can seek Him even when I am under the false impression that I am the one in control of my own happiness. When things are good and my kids are behaving and my pocketbook is fat and I don't have leukemia, I can still remember where all that good stuff comes from. My tendency is to tell God, "*Thankyouverymuch* for helping me through that FastPass line. You just take a little break and I'll take over for a bit." But what He wants is for me to stay as close to Him in the regular line as I do in the FastPass line. Truly, I want that too. Unfortunately, it takes a lot more effort than when I am acutely aware of my inability to control my own life. When standing in the regular line, depending on Him, is, as the recovery saying goes, "Easy to do-easy not to do." But maybe, just maybe, if I applied that desperate seeking and trusting and crying out in my everyday life, I could become that wiser, kinder, inspiring person without having to wait for a FastPass in order to get there.

Just a thought ...

"In this world you will have trouble. But take heart! I have OVERCOME (hammered, licked, crucified, demolished, overpowered, thrashed, conquered, defeated, routed, beaten) the world" (John 16:33)

Squatters

Even if you are not a Bible scholar, there's a good possibility that you have heard the story about Jesus' parents leaving him behind when they headed home from their vacation. They actually traveled for an entire day before they realized he was missing (let's just pause to contemplate how even though my parenting could use some work, I have never left a child alone in another city for an entire day). In all fairness, they traveled in a type of caravan with many other families and relatives. They probably assumed he was with Uncle Joe in the back of the pack.

I secretly suspect that his brothers knew full well he wasn't there but imagine the stress of living with the perfect Son of God as your brother! Who could blame them for looking the other way when they pulled out of town without him? When Jesus' absence was finally noticed, they turned around and headed back to Jerusalem to look for him. When they found him, he was in the temple, sitting among the teachers, listening to them and asking them questions. When his parents saw him they were astonished and I suspect, just a little irritated. Mary said, "Son, why have you treated us like this? Your father and I have been anxiously searching for you." And Jesus answered them like any teenager would, "Why were you searching for me? Didn't you know I had to be in my Father's house?" (Luke 2:49).

This is the thought that came to me: Do I look upon my life as being in my Father's House? Here's what I believe to be true about God--He created me to dwell in His House. His Will. With His Spirit occupying my being. It's the most natural place for me to be. But more often than not, I am trying to move my stuff into other people's houses.

In Las Vegas, over the past few years, they have had a terrible problem with "squatters." A squatter is someone who occupies real property that they have no legal right or title to live in. What's crazy is that if a squatter enters a vacant home and manages to get the electricity turned on through the city, it will take lawyers and owners thousands of dollars and dozens of hours to get them out. Truly, the best, and most challenging way to get the house back is if they leave on their own accord. But who would do that when they are living in a beautiful house in a gated community

... for FREE? (Never mind the fact that their neighbors despise them and they are under the daily threat of being kicked out!)

When we put down our roots and organize our belongings in any other house but our Father's House, we become squatters. We were not designed to live outside our Father's Will. You may move your stuff in, but it will never feel like HOME. We need to live in the moment in our Father's House. It's where we belong.

Oh, ye of little faith

I am not positive that at the end of this entry, I will actually post it for anyone else to read. I just need to get some things out of my head. First, I have to admit that I have done it again--believed the lie that plagues me: "Unless I am currently living in peace, love, forgiveness, joy and hope, I have no right to write." Who really wants to hear from someone who is battling fear and resentment and doubt? I guess that's not really a question for me to answer. My job is just to put it out there. If nothing else, it might help me.

I am completely out of control. And I mean that literally. Not the "running wild" out of control, just fresh out of any ability to control (as if I ever had it in the first place). I probably don't need to say much more than just state the fact that I have a 20-year-old college student who lives in California, a 16-year-old son who just got his license and a 15-year-old daughter getting ready to start public high school. And one husband. When my kids were little, I fooled myself into believing that how I was raising them and steering them would produce certain results and that I was responsible for the outcome. Silly me. You see this silliness when "perfect parenting" results in rebellious teens and absent or abusive parenting produces Olympic athletes or valedictorians. This reminds me that I can only do so much. It reminds me that God does not have grandchildren, He has children. I am His child, and my kids are His children. Not once removed. A direct link to God and His specific plan for them.

If I have so little control over my immediate family, why do I live with anxiety and fear because I feel unable to control every other part of my world? I am a real estate agent. When I am living in trust and faith that God is in control, that He sees my circumstances and that He has a good plan, I can drive around town like a normal person. But when I get to thinking that I am in charge of other people's decisions to buy or sell houses, every single "For Sale" sign I see causes me to doubt myself and dare I say, feel the tiniest bit jealous or resentful that my name is not on that sign. This fear is an indication that I think I know better than God what should be happening in my business.

Let's see--we have covered kids, spouses, jobs ... what else is plaguing me? Oh yes--money. Yep, I admit it, I fret about this. I worry about my kids having jobs (trying to control them) and if I will sell enough houses (trying to control the entire real estate market) and how long we can continue to pay for everything (trying to control my financial security).

This is just the superficial stuff. I haven't even touched on how badly I want control of everyone's moral and spiritual choices. How I want to be able to produce character and responsible behavior in my kids.

I go to a Recovery program for family or friends of those who have been affected by the disease of alcoholism. But, we work the same twelve steps as the alcoholics. Why? Because, as you have witnessed above, we all have our own "isms" that interfere with our chances of living in freedom and joy. My "ism" is "control-ism." So I have to start with the first step and insert my "ism": "We admitted we were powerless over people, places and things--that our lives had become unmanageable."[10] I read in one of my readings today, specifically on control, that "trying to be in control is an effective method of keeping loved ones at a distance." It sure is. My family doesn't want to engage with me when I am in control mode. It alienates. It robs them of their dignity. It does the exact opposite of what I am intending to do.

Fear. Anxiety. Worry. Those are the feelings I live with when I believe the lie that I have power over people, places, or things. I hate feeling this way. My only solution is to turn "my will and my life over to the care of God as I understand Him."[11] To have faith that He is the only one in control and He knows better than I do what is best for everyone I love.

"Why are you fearful, oh ye of little faith?"
Matthew 8:26

(Thanks for listening ☺)

Common sense

Over the summer, I have occasionally noticed a little boy riding his bike past my house. Well, I am not sure if it is his own bike, as it is about two sizes too big for him. He has to stand up to ride it. It looks dangerous and dare I say, risky, should he plan to produce children someday (if you catch my drift!). We happen to have a bike that no longer gets ridden. A boy's bike, just about his size. Every time I see this boy, the thought occurs to me that maybe he would like to have it. That maybe it could be used and enjoyed, rather than collect dust in my garage. But I have never acted on that thought, until Tuesday.

I was sitting in my living room and this same boy rode by my window on not only a too-big bike, but a PINK bike. It took me about a minute before the thought came to me again that maybe he would like to have our bike. I jumped up and ran outside but he was nowhere to be found. He had completely disappeared. I walked down to the intersection at the end of the block and looked in all directions. Nothing. As I turned around to walk home, I asked God for a sign. "God, if you want me to give him this bike, have him show up before I go back in my house" (but I did throw out the possibility that I might still do it, even if he didn't show up in the next couple minutes. As you can see, I had great confidence that God would answer ...).

As I approached my house, I turned around one last time, and here he came. He rolled up on the pink bike and crossed over to my side of the street. Riding straight toward my house. Straight toward me. He didn't really even seem surprised or uncomfortable about me asking him to stop. Or about the fact that, in a nutshell, I told him that I felt like God was telling me to give him the bike. (As a rule, I would encourage my child to run from such a person.) We agreed he would talk to his mom about it and come back this weekend to ride it and see if it was something he wanted. He said "thankyouverymuch" and left.

So here's the part that disturbs me--even though I asked God for a sign, a very specific sign, when He answered it in less than five minutes' time and exactly as I requested, I still doubted if this was actually from Him. I still faltered on if He really wanted me to give this boy the bike. I mean, it was an expensive bike, after all. Maybe his parents don't want him to have his own bike for some reason. Maybe I am interfering to make myself feel better about having too much stuff. Maybe he likes riding his big brother's or sister's bike!

All these thoughts ran through my head immediately after God answered my prayer. As requested, in record time. That's messed up. I don't believe God reacts like I do to these types of things, but if He did, I imagine He would be pulling His hair out in frustration, saying, "Seriously, Heather?"

A couple things come to mind as I try to understand myself on this. One--when I can't accept God's power and ability to influence my daily life, I have enthroned common sense. Oswald Chambers says, "Every time you venture out in the life of faith, you will find something in your common-sense circumstances that flatly contradicts your faith. Common sense is not faith, and faith is not common sense."[12] No, it does not make sense to me, or to that little boy, that I would give a perfect stranger an expensive bike because God told me to do it. But it's also pretty hard to make what happened prior to that fit in the common-sense category either.

Perhaps you have had some of those moments. Moments where you just "know-in-your-knower" you are supposed to take an action; pay someone's bill, send someone a specific text of encouragement that doesn't make sense to you, call a friend you haven't talked to in years, tell someone you forgive them or scarier yet, ask them to forgive you. I guess my fear for myself is that if I can almost talk myself out of an action that you and I both know was pretty darn clear, how often do I talk myself out of less obvious things God is prompting me to do?

My second thought is this: Am I so afraid of what others will think of me that I choose to disobey God? Sometimes the answer is "yes." I don't really want to be labeled a "Jesus-Freak" or a "weirdo." And if it makes me the tiniest bit uncomfortable, it's just easier to tell myself that I am just being impulsive and write it off as a crazy thought.

Or maybe, just maybe, living according to what God directs me to do is how I live the adventure that His way of life offers. Living any other way is boring, or should I say "Common."

Common sense: Part 2

The answer is "no", or "not yet." He did not come to get his bike this weekend. When I wrote Common sense Part 1, I didn't want to bore you with more than 750 words at once so I decided to wait until today (I also may have forgotten until later that night ...). Here's the rest of what I wanted to say ...

Even though we act on a prompting from God, it doesn't give us the right to expect the results to live up to our expectations. Would I have loved it if that boy had shown up for the bike with a joyful spirit and a big smile and thanked me with a hug before he happily rode down the street? Of course. *But I am not in control of that part of the story.* All I can control is whether or not I listen. Whether or not I act. How it turns out is neither here nor there.

It doesn't mean that God wasn't in it. It doesn't mean that I did it wrong. It even occurs to me that it might not have anything to do with that boy or the bike at all. Maybe it was a moment between me and God where He made it clear to me that He heard me, He can answer me in specifics if I ask Him to, and that He's personally invested in our relationship. His promises are not generic. They are meant for me and He speaks to me in unique ways because I am a unique girl (no comments, please). He speaks to you too. He will speak the words and use the tone that He knows will get your attention.

So, again, I don't have an answer to report to you regarding the bike. And that's OK. It isn't necessary for me to SEE the answer. My job is to obey and then trust God with the results.

Scary stories

I am about to reveal some frightening things about myself. You've been warned. They are embarrassing to put on paper, but I feel like they illustrate a point worth making, so I will sacrifice my reputation to help us all learn something. (And I feel like it's only fair to let you know what you are up against should you choose to leave the safety of your own home after reading this.) Here we go ...

The first confession is by far the worst: One day I was making an apple pie while I was home alone. When I went to add the cinnamon, I couldn't find it anywhere (even though I was certain I had just bought a brand new bottle). As I got ready to run to Walgreens to get more, after searching the entire house for cinnamon, I remembered that my in-laws were in town and had taken my car to run errands. I thought about taking my bike then remembered it was at the shop getting a new tire. Since the shop is only about a half mile from my house, I decided I would just walk to the bike shop, ride to the store for cinnamon and come home and finish my pie. So, I got my keys, went to my car, and got my wallet out of my purse and proceeded to walk to the bike shop. (At this point, if you are not saying "huh?" in your head, you should probably stay home today for your own safety and that of others.) Yes, you read that right. I got my wallet *out of my CAR and walked to the bike shop because I had no CAR* to drive to the store. The scariest part is that it didn't even come together in my head until I was pulling in my driveway after I rode my bike to the store for cinnamon. Sigh. It's just so humiliating. I didn't tell anyone at all for a few weeks. I couldn't bear to admit that my brain had completely shut down like that.

That one was a doozy. The others are milder and spread out over the years, but here are just a few examples of what happens when there is no "ZZZT" going on in my brain: I once left my car running the entire time I was with my kids while they ate and played in the tubes in McDonalds Playland (even though I had gone to my car to get something out of it about halfway through). Another time, as I went into church, my husband Blake reminded me to shut the doors to the van but instead of shutting one I apparently opened the other with my key remote, leaving both doors wide open as it poured rain for the next hour.

A couple of years ago, I got the mail, looked through it and for some reason set it on top of my car. One envelope contained a large check, and it blew away in the cul de sac as I headed out for our Christmas Eve service. We didn't realize it was missing until my husband asked about it the next morning, after it had snowed about four inches. I spent Christmas morning digging around in the snow looking for WHITE envelopes! I am happy to say that they were recovered but after much emotional turmoil and cold, manual labor. (As I was writing this, my sweet husband came home for lunch. Blake kindly reminded me, after I told him about the stories I was telling on myself, that on that same Christmas Eve I had gotten out of the car as it began to snow and my cell phone fell off my lap, unnoticed. So on Christmas Day we also drove around the church parking lot calling my phone until we found it--intact and frozen. I think I must have blocked that all out--way too much to handle...) And just yesterday, I seriously almost backed over the "cart-boy" at the grocery store because the sun was making a glare on my backup camera in my car and I couldn't see him. It did not even occur to me to look out the actual window, like a normal person, until I saw him leaping out of the way and "flagging" me on. What in the world??????

So, lest this be the last of my blogs you ever read, let's just throw out a lesson or two that might redeem such terrifying stories. I think most of us have done things like search the house for our glasses/sunglasses, only to find them on top of our head (please say "yes" or I am in worse trouble than I thought). But my examples are the result of a bigger problem than being blonde or spacey. For me, they are a direct indication of my mind being preoccupied with worry or stress or fear.

When my mind is focused on those things, the space left over for rational, logical, engaged thinking becomes very tiny. The fixation on trying to make sense of or manage an unmanageable situation takes over my mind so that everyday menial tasks become too much for me to handle. I forget things. I can't put two and two together. I almost kill people!

A reminder I hear regularly from a wise person in my life is to "keep my head with my hands." This way no one gets hurt. My instructions are: If I am driving, I focus on driving. If my kids are talking to me, I actually listen and don't pretend to be listening while my thoughts are worried about other things. If I am working out, I focus on the task at hand. If I am with one friend, I don't let my mind be distracted by the hurt caused by a different friend. Fretting and stewing about people, places, and things while I am trying to "live" my life, keeps me from experiencing the joy of the moment and can be downright dangerous to myself and others.

So there you have it. *Scary Stories* by Heather Carter. Please, for the love of Pete, let it help you in some way, because that was painful. (By the way, about a month later my friend brought me a bottle of cinnamon I had apparently taken to her house to dust my pineapple with. I am not sure if this information helps or hurts my case. ☺)

...On "morning" in the morning

"Morning--the very word itself is like a cluster of luscious grapes to crush into sacred wine for me to drink. In the morning! This is when God wants me at my best in strength and hope so that I may begin my daily climb, not in weakness but in strength. Last night I buried yesterday's fatigue, and this morning I took on a new supply of energy. Blessed is the day when the morning is sanctified--set apart to God! Successful is the day when the first victory is won in prayer! Holy is the day when the dawn finds me on the mountaintop with God!" (L.B. Cowman)[13]

If your reaction to that reading is "Amen Sista!", you are what we call a "morning person." If, on the other hand, that reading (if you can even see it clearly through the sleepiness lingering in your fuzzy eyes) makes you feel slightly nauseous and possibly even guilty that you don't share those sentiments, you are what we call "not a morning person." You know who you are, one way or another.

Recently, my husband told me he read an article that the most successful people get up at approximately 4:30 a.m. every day. I have many thoughts on that, but I will keep them to myself.

My daughter is one of those "not a morning person" people. She is 15 and until this year, she would emerge from her bedroom each morning with her "blankie" over her head. She would leave enough of a hole for her to see through as she poured her cereal and headed back to her room and shut the door.

Perhaps some of you are like my oldest son who shares Ryan Howard's (from the *Office* TV show) thoughts on being outside at the crack of dawn with his co-workers: "Ever since I've gotten clean, there's something about fresh morning air ... that just really makes me sick."

So, you might be wondering what I am ... Well, I am going to tell you anyway ...

I am both. Or neither. However you want to look at it. I really really HATE the initial getting out of bed. I immediately start fantasizing about when I can get back in bed or take a nap later that day. I make coffee, stagger to the couch, and pick up my books that I read to get my day started. Much of the time I don't really feel like reading or thinking or praying. But I do it anyway. Not because I am super-spiritual because I am certainly not. More likely, it is because I am a broken, selfish, scatterbrained girl whose only hope is to at least start off on the right foot. Sadly, by the time I head out the door I have put much of what I read in the past and moved on without even considering what I learned that morning. It's a problem, really.

For years and years I was rigid about this practice. And if I missed a day--look out! The guilt and disappointment in myself went wild. I was missing the whole point. And what is that point, you might be asking? The point is not to check it off your list or be able to present a perfect attendance record before God or others for approval; the point is to "give God the fresh blossom of the day. Never make Him wait until the petals have faded."[14]

When I begin my day reflecting on the blessings, the fears, the stresses, the failures, and the anticipation of the day ahead, and then *turn them over to God first thing (in the morning)*, I have a fighting chance of living in some sort of serenity. It's so much better than waiting until all hell has broken loose and I feel like I am going to lose my mind. By then it's almost too late. Or at least much harder to recover from. Starting my day with God is like preventive care for my soul.

So even when every fiber of my being wants to just lie down on the couch and go back to sleep--I read. I pray. I prepare for what is to come. I don't know about your life, but my life is hard every day. Not because of circumstances, but because it's just plain hard to live in this world with serenity and joy and with a mindfulness of God's ways over my ways. At the very least, maybe start by acknowledging God while your head's on your pillow. Start your day at least pointed in His general direction. See how it goes ...

Super-stuck

Even before the pastor started preaching on worry and how to get "UNSTUCK", I had found my card they give us to write notes on at church and starting venting: "I am ***super-stuck***. Stuck in a pattern of anxiety about things in my life that I can't control. I am freakin' afraid! Afraid that my kids, my marriage, my job, my health will all fail. I feel haunted. Joyless. STUCK. *Unable to move freely in my days and into my future.* Paralyzed." Now, if that's not a fine spiritual posture to have as a sermon starts, I don't know what is!

While he was preaching about being stuck, I remembered a scary, and embarrassing, time that I got myself stuck when I was little. I was young enough that I honestly can't remember my motives for doing this, but I, for some brilliant reason, put my small hand inside the opening of one of those gumball machines at the grocery store. It was the kind that dispersed the plastic ball filled with some worthless little trinket. So the mouth was pretty large and my hand seemed like it would fit perfectly up there. Like I said, I would like to say that I did it because I had put my money in and nothing came out or else the trinket was stuck. I hope that's the case. But I guess it's just as likely that my mom told me, "No, you can't buy that stupid piece of junk," and so I decided that maybe I could just get it myself by sticking my hand up there. Regardless, my point is that my little hand got stuck and there was soon a team of employees surrounding me, trying to help me get it out. Fantastic.

One thing that my pastor pointed out while I was daydreaming about my trauma from the gumball machine incident, is that "it's easier to get stuck than it is to get unstuck." Got that straight! In order to get unstuck, and these are my personal reflections based on said incident, there are two major things you need to do:

1) **RELAX**. Stop struggling. If you fight or flail or panic, you will only make the problem worse. Sounds sort of like "Be still and know that I am God" to me. Sometimes I get stuck because I make bad choices or try to get what I want before it's time to get it. Sometimes, like right now, I get stuck because I want to control the uncontrollable. I can't just relax and let God take care of it. I push and shove and manipulate to get my way and end up stuck in my fear and anxiety. I have to stop trying to fix it and just rest and trust.

2) **LET GO**. I can't get unstuck from a gumball machine if my fist is wrapped around, clinging to, the plastic treat inside. It's impossible. I could try all day long and the physics of it just doesn't work out. I am currently clinging to my kids, my husband, my job, my future, and my health with all my might. Well, I am trying, anyway. These are items that no one can actually hold. So why do I spend so much energy trying to do so? I have to LET GO of the things I am hoping to manage and LET GOD have them and take care of them. It sounds too good to be true. Too simple to be the answer for a smart girl or boy like me or you. But we can either do a really bad job of doing God's job, or we can let Him do it. Let Him have it. Even if I take it and give it back a hundred times a day.

I am doing Step 3 in my Recovery Program this month. The last lines of what I read every day coincides suspiciously well with what God might be trying to teach me from every angle (I need constant reminders, as my brain has a slow leak...): "We place ourselves in a position in which, no matter what happens in our lives, we can trust that we will be guided and cared for. We are no longer in charge. By placing ourselves in the care of the God of our understanding, we put ourselves in much more capable hands."[15]

Today you only have 2 things to do: RELAX. LET GO.

What a relief!

I only have 15 minutes to put my thoughts on "paper" before I have to head to an appointment. But I just don't think I can wait until I get home to write. It keeps writing itself in my head. Last night, as I spoke the words out loud, I remembered something I had forgotten to remember: there is a big difference between Relief and Solution (I know you must feel great *relief* knowing that I am going to finally clear this up for you ☺).

Relief: "The feeling of reassurance and relaxation following release from anxiety or distress" (Merriam-Webster Dictionary). It's a wonderful feeling when the pressure valve of our emotions has been opened and we can just feel the steam escaping. Deflating us back down to our normal, sane, stable selves. I love that feeling. Some ways that this can happen for me, and maybe for you, are by talking (venting) to a safe, close friend or by attending a group that allows me to puke all the emotions out to people who have been through something similar.

Those are pretty healthy ways to get relief. And often necessary for me so I don't explode. Sometimes it might look like me screaming at the top of my lungs at God, going for a walk in nature, sitting in the hot tub, or even taking a nap. (Some of you might say you go for a hard run to get some relief. Just thinking about running gives me anxiety so that would be a "no" for me!)

Again. These are all good things to get some relief for feelings that have risen out of circumstances that are stressing me out. Maybe, like me, you also do some things that aren't quite as good. Oh, they *feel* good, for sure. I really like them because they are quick to affect me. Things like having a glass of wine to take the "edge" off, shopping for something I don't need, or eating (I was going to say ice cream, but really you can just insert your own "go-to" food of sinful proportions for this illustration).

While these may help us feel less anxious immediately, they ultimately are not a good, final answer to our anxiety, and often produce some extra emotions to deal with (shame, guilt, regret, etc.). Even in the dictionary the word relief is also defined as "a TEMPORARY break in a generally tense or tedious situation."

So (in five minutes or less), the alternative is SOLUTION. When you seek a solution to something, you use a "particular method of solving; an explanation or answer" (Merriam-Webster Dictionary). This is an answer to WHY you are feeling so anxious. A solution helps you get to the root of your need for relief. If it is used right, it can be permanent. In math, if you solve the problem once with a certain equation, you can solve that same problem the next time by using the exact same equation. It's not complicated after that initial "working out of the problem."

When I looked up the definition of solution (and I love it when this happens!), I found an interesting definition hidden under how it is used in medical terms. It says, "the termination of a disease" (Merriam-Webster Dictionary). And isn't that what we suffer from? Anxiety, worry, constant fear and intimidation and lack of confidence and on and on it goes. But that is the good news, people. There IS a solution to this "disease" that has plagued us, possibly since birth. And alcohol, drugs, food, sex, exercise, overachieving, shopping and YOU, are not IT.

I know it sounds almost too simple to believe, but God and His ways are IT. He asks us to live, trusting HIM and letting HIM be in control. This is the solution to anxiety. He asks us to forgive others the way He forgave us and love those who harm us. This is our SOLUTION to hate and resentment. He asks us not to fret about tomorrow but live in today. This is our SOLUTION to fear of the future and regret over our past. He asks us to love and serve those around us, especially using our brokenness to do so. This is our SOLUTION to self-pity. He asks us to "count it all JOY when we face trials of many kinds" (James 1:2). This is our SOLUTION to despair.

I could go on, but I am already going to have to throw on some sweats and put a hat over my crazy hair and head to an appointment! But as you can tell, the proposition of seeking and finding a SOLUTION excites me. Relief is good and necessary sometimes, but it doesn't last. I am tired of trying to find new ways to put a Band-Aid on a gushing wound. The only way to stop the bleeding once and for all is to find a SOLUTION. May you seek and find yours today.

A blog about nothing

Don't worry. I am in no way implying that my mind thinks like the brilliant and hilarious Jerry Seinfeld. *But*, I do have to say that I remind myself of him in one particular area: we both have managed to create something out of nothing. When Jerry Seinfeld and George Costanza pitched their idea for a sitcom to NBC they told them, "It's a show about NOTHING." When asked what *happens* in this show, George emphatically tells them, "NOTHING happens ... what did you do today?" NBC: "I got up and came to work." George: "There's a show! THAT'S a show!" And for nine seasons they managed to sustain a cult following for a "show about nothing." When people ask me what I write about, the answer is sort of the same. NOTHING. Or maybe a better answer is EVERYTHING. Everywhere I go, events and people trigger thoughts that make me NEED to write a blog about it. I can't stop myself. And in that vein, I give you ... in Seinfeld fashion ...THE DENTIST. (Don't worry, if you watch Seinfeld it is in no way similar to the DENTIST episode. So you can relax. ☺)

Remember when I was rushing to finish my last blog? I had to go get a cavity filled. Up until the past five years, my kids have been blessed to see a dentist who is a family friend. When our life flipped upside down, we had to change many things, and that was one of them. New house, new job, new friends, new schools, new church, new doctor, new *dentist.* And while we are on the dental subject, I should confess that I have pretty deep-seated issues with dentists. It's possible it started when I was little and had to get a filling.

According to my mother, I got very nervous and, either accidentally or on purpose, kicked the nice dentist in his most delicate parts. Only he wasn't very nice after that and that scared me too. Apparently, the dentist thought I did it intentionally, because after the visit he gave my mother her very own copy of "Dare to Discipline" by James Dobson. Ever since that episode, I have sat in the dentist chair with trepidation.

Everything changed when I stepped into Renken Dentistry. Even the name of this place rolls off my tongue like I am going to the spa. My kids actually look forward to going to the dentist now! It's crazy. When they lead you through the doors to your appointment, they chat happily while Mumford or Adele or the Eagles play in the background. All the employees, every last one of them, are chipper and has "smiley" eyes that peek over their masks while they clean your teeth.

We talk about prom dresses and crock pot cooking and our favorite flavor of tooth polish. I have had a few fillings there as well as a root canal. I can tell that one of their main goals is to take any apprehension out of the dental visit. I know they sense my fears (as I cling to the arms of the chair) because they ask me repeatedly if I am feeling OK and if it hurts and then praise me for doing a good job when it's over. I remember hearing (and if you are a dentist, please don't take offense at this) that dentists have a tendency toward depression directly related to the job they do. Let's face it, not many people *like* going to the dentist. Whether or not that's true, it seems like it would make sense if it were.

Now, to get to the point ... the difference between my "dental spa" and other dental offices is their approach. Their attitude. They still give me shots and drill and floss. That is the same. But because of their philosophy of dispelling people's fears and exuding a happy, positive spirit, I always leave there feeling uplifted. So, I ask myself and you--can we try to live that way too? Would it kill us to try to approach our unpleasant circumstances with this same spirit?

Let's face it, life is hard. It thoroughly sucks on some days. And even if YOUR day is going well, chances are that others are suffering. What would happen in our world if we addressed the fact that people are generally as apprehensive about their lives as they are about going to the dentist? Maybe YOUR approach, your positivity, your smile as you open the door for a stranger, could help them move forward with a lighter spirit. If it can happen at a DENTIST office ...

*And there you go: A BLOG ABOUT NOTHING. "There's a blog! THAT'S a blog!"

Great expectations

My daughter is reading *Great Expectations* (by Charles Dickens). Don't tell her teacher, but she hates it. Not the story, necessarily. She actually likes the plot. It's the long pages of wordiness and tedious talk that is about to make her go crazy. She spends way too much time reading me excerpts to prove how dull it is. I agree with her. The book, and the topic, are complicated. Expectations, in general, are like that.

I think there is no better time to talk about EXPECTATIONS than around one's birthday. I feel like this has notoriously been a time when I set myself up for some major disappointment if I don't have my expectations in check. Birthday celebrations are really important to me. Specifically, MY birthday celebration is really important to me. And more specifically, how my family behaves, responds, and treats me all day long on MY birthday is really important to me. I probably don't have to tell you that this leads to some disappointing birthday "celebrations." It's not because my family doesn't love me or appreciate me on this momentous day. I always get gifts and cards and a dinner out at some point during my birthday week. I realize that is more than a lot of other people get. But my expectations are so high that I am pretty sure that most humans could not even begin to fill my "birthday-shaped" chasm of neediness on this one day.

This year I finally wised up. I finally faced the fact that my expectations were setting me up for serious resentments. So I did what any smart girl would do under the circumstances; I called my momma! Of all the people I knew to spend time with on my birthday, I knew she had the capacity to exceed my expectations. So, I arranged to spend the day with her and even stay overnight at her house about an hour away. My dad knew that it was best to just "stay out of our way" so he came here and helped manage the kids and their schedules. Mom and I ate and shopped and ate again and went to the movies in the middle of a Thursday and then went home and watched another movie while she rubbed my feet! It was perfect.

Someone once said that "an expectation is a premeditated resentment." We know that some people are incapable of following through, yet for some reason we expect them to show up and even be there on time. We are disappointed. We have experienced stressful, chaotic holiday dinners year after year, yet this year we expect that maybe they will be different. We are disappointed. We expect tenderness or understanding or affection from a spouse who does not have it in them to give. We are disappointed. We expect (and this is a big one) our kids to say thank you for providing a nice meal, doing their laundry, or running to the store for the last-minute item for the project they forgot about. We are disappointed. We expect people in general to be respectful to us. To be kind to all. To be patient. To behave like we think they should. We are majorly disappointed.

I used to get very put out when someone would suggest my expectations were too high. That I should lower them. What I have come to learn is that there is a difference between expectations and standards. And more importantly, I have no right to impose either of them on other people. Even when I have high standards for how I behave and how I allow others to treat me, it doesn't always mean that I should expect those to be met. Sometimes there are really good reasons why they can't be. I can be compassionate when this happens. And I can accept the reality of what others are able to give. They say the level of disappointment we live with is directly related to the distance between our expectations and reality. Lowering, or adjusting, my expectations of others doesn't mean I have to accept unacceptable behavior. It's a way of taking care of my own soul and preventing those premeditated resentments.

(Stay tuned for the expectations we put on ourselves. Those are even more brutal!)

Greater expectations

If I have Great Expectations of others, I have even Greater Expectations of myself. Where I am apt to extend grace and understanding to others if they fall short, my go-to reaction to my own shortcomings is anything but. I was talking (read: whining) to my sponsor the other day about just such a response to myself. This usually happens when I "should" on myself: "I should be better, stronger, thinner, happier, richer and definitely more spiritual, more motivated, more joyful, more peaceful and more loving by now!" I am not sure why "now" is when I "should" be all those things, except that my expectations of what my circumstances and my character should look like might be a tad bid too high. Too unrealistic.

Perhaps some of these expectations are created when I compare my insides with other people's outsides. Or, as I heard author Steven Furtick say, I am "comparing my behind the scenes with someone else's highlight reel."[16]

The comparison game ends in despair and discouragement. In a reading from *Courage to Change*, it suggests that maybe it would "be better to compare our present circumstances only to where we had been in the past."[17] We are aiming for progress, not perfection. Shaming ourselves and beating ourselves up when we don't perform like others, who have entirely different personalities, wiring, and life circumstances is, well, ridiculous. We would NEVER tell someone else that they "should" be able to have the kind of perspective that a person who is dying has. We would NEVER think of suggesting that someone strive to look like a Cross-Fit Champion a few weeks after they started working out for the first time. We would NEVER think to reprimand a friend who struggles with depression or motivation. But for some reason we think it's OK to hold ourselves to these unrealistic standards and flog ourselves when we don't measure up. When it comes to ME, I tend to expect perfection, rather than celebrate progress.

But as a good friend always reminds me, "I don't have to live that way anymore." Today, I can give myself a break. Cut myself some slack. I can quit playing the comparison game. I can be gentle with myself. I can celebrate how far I have come. I can give time, *time* and keep moving in the right direction. Each of us is doing the best we can with what we have been given. And though that might not be where we want to land, just for today, ***it's enough***.

Elongate your stride

I am completely back-blogged! I have so many topics rolling around in my head that I can barely decide which one to put on paper today. I think, since I am starting a new workout regimen (read: "getting off my rear after about a month of NOT working out"), I will write about running. Don't get excited. I am NOT running today. Just a nice walk in the park. But as I have mentioned in other blogs, I used to be a runner. Or, maybe that is a little strong. I wasn't really a "runner" per se, I just ran two half-marathons in about two months. (Mainly because one of them was a DIVA run in California for my sister-in-law's 40th birthday. I'll do just about anything to get to California in December. Even RUN.) After I crossed the finish line, I quit my running career because my body was in revolt.

BUT, when I was training for said half-marathons, I started cold turkey. I went from NEVER running in August, to doing a race in October and one in December. I had to learn fast and train hard. I knew

I couldn't do this by myself. I joined a running group and did my best to copy what they were doing. They were *real* runners, after all. I chose a couple ladies about my age who were about my same build, plugged in my headphones and ... stalked them. I would get right behind them and try to keep up with them. It's sort of a running joke in my family that I have a very short stride.

When we go to amusement parks or do any kind of walking as a family, I practically have to skip to keep up with even my "little" children. My husband instructs, "Elongate your stride!" So, it goes without saying that mimicking the stride of an *actual* runner was a huge stretch for me. It was hard and very uncomfortable. I had to push myself.

Today, in my Oswald Chambers book, I read, "In learning to walk with God there is always the difficulty of getting into His ***stride*** ... it is difficult to get into stride with God, because when we start walking with Him we find He has outstripped us before we have taken three steps. He has different ways of doing things, and we have to be trained and disciplined into His ways."[18] Sometimes, especially at first, or when we are distracted, it is challenging to follow in His ways.

Sometimes it's like me following those runners; I start off close and manage to stay in step, but occasionally I fall behind or get out of sync with their stride or start looking at the scenery and forget that

I am supposed to be following someone. I am not sure if the girls ahead of me could sense my magnetic presence behind them. But God does. His hope is that I not only follow, but that I fall in stride right next to Him. As I followed/stalked those girls week after week, I eventually caught up, introduced myself, and we became running buddies.

God longs for us to be His running buddies. God doesn't have to prove how awesome He is by showing off (His awesomeness is already well-established), staying just enough ahead of me to make Himself look fast and me feel slow. As we "run" with God, His "Spirit alters the atmosphere of our way of looking at things, and things begin to be possible which never were possible before. Getting into the STRIDE of God means nothing less than union with Himself. It takes a long time to get there, but keep at it. Don't give in because the pain is bad just now, get on with it, and before long you will find you have a new vision and a new purpose."[19]

On that note--I am going for a nice *walk*.

One and two and...

I was reading something last night before bed, and it reminded me of something I did this weekend. I have to tell you, I am so pleased about it because this is a story that needs to be told and I just never knew how to tell it--until now. So, bear with me as I start this from the beginning ...

A few months ago I felt that I was supposed to rejoin the worship/singing team at church. It's been about six years since I have sung in front of people and on a microphone. I am out of practice and, well, OLD. I was feeling very intimidated. The first time went as well as it could for my first time back (I didn't choke or come out with my dress tucked into my underwear or anything). The second time I sang I was having a bit of trouble learning my part so I went to the office and met with the worship director. He helped me and then said, "Now, you did notice on the order of service that I have you playing the synth?" I calmly replied, "You are aware that I don't play any kind of keyboard, right?" He blew it off and said, "You'll be fine."

So I practiced and practiced for my "synth debut." Singing was not even on my radar after that. I was laser-focused on my synth part. I couldn't even sing while I played. That would for sure throw me off. The next time I sang he put me on the "chain." Yes, a large chain that you might pull a car out a ditch with. Again, I practiced and practiced dropping and lifting that chain like my life depended on it. And then came this last weekend: The Humidor. You read that right. Only this time he took it up a notch and had me play one rhythm with my left hand (ONE and two

AND three and four and) and another with a stick in my right hand (1-2-3-4-5-6-7-8). For those of you not musically inclined, those are two *entirely* different rhythms with two different instruments, and one of them is on the OFF beat. Translation: really hard to do if you aren't an actual percussionist. It's like rubbing your belly and patting your head at the same time.

I have to say, I am starting to believe that the powers that be really aren't a fan of my singing voice but don't have the heart to tell me. Maybe they are hoping I'll put my foot down and quit (but they don't know who they are dealing with!). I can imagine them thinking, "Bless her heart ... She can't really sing, so let's just give her something to do up there so she doesn't feel bad and won't be able to sing while she's doing it."

Here's how I made it through this weekend's Humidor Challenge: when it was time to jump in on my beat, I stared like a stalker at the drummer. He was sort of on the same kind of rhythm as me and I found that if I really focused and did not try to sing or engage in anything else that was happening in the service, I was able to stay on track. If I ever considered trying to look like I was relaxed and casual and possibly tried to sing a note or two, all was lost. It was like playing double-Dutch jump rope trying to come back in if I got lost or off the beat.

So, 594 words later, you might be asking, "And what is your point, exactly?" Well, here's what my reading by author Sarah Young said to me (this is supposed to be God talking ...), "If you focus on the obstacle or search for a way around it, you will probably go off course. Instead, FOCUS ON ME (capitalization mine), the Shepherd who is leading you along your life-journey."[20] I have been battling with this so much lately. My fretting and worrying and trying to control the outcome of every activity I take part in is literally making me feel crazy.

When I read that, I was reminded of how I had to focus on the drummer to stay on beat, to keep the rhythm. In order to prevent my mind and heart from being distracted from God's plan for me and others, I have to have "stalker" focus on HIM at all times. Trusting that HE knows better than I do what is best for me and other people. Praying for HIS will to be done in my life and the lives of others, not for Him to give me what I think is best. I have been forgetting that He has a plan, and it's a good one. It's the best one. And I don't have to know exactly what it is in order to live with serenity.

God says to me, "Although you remain aware of the visible world around you, your primary awareness needs to be of Me."[21]

Dear God, help me to be hyper-focused on YOU, just like I was on that drummer. Following Your rhythm for my life, even as distractions swirl around me, will protect me from the fear, anxiety, and fretting that plague me when my eyes wander off to lesser things.

Me too

I was driving down the street, worrying, fretting, and feeling overwhelmed with life in general, when out of nowhere I heard a voice. I was pretty sure it wasn't God's voice because the message wasn't very nice. I heard it loud and clear: "I liked you better when you had cancer." Before I could answer, "Me too," it dawned on me that I was alone in the car. It was my own voice. A true, but distressing message that had been building in my heart for quite some time. So now it was out there. Now I had no choice but to address the why behind the insanity of preferring cancer over remission. Even as I sit here processing, I am not sure what I am going to say. I have never explored it fully. Mostly I have joked about needing to go to the hospital to get some rest from regular life. I haven't really thought through the reality that I miss the ME I was when I had leukemia. OK (deep breath/staring out the window/praying/asking for insight/feeling the feelings/remembering) ...

... Let's start with the most obvious and simple reason. Number One: I was nicer. At least I felt nicer. I let go of expectations of other people and just took what God brought me with an open hand. When I was in the hospital (some 70 days total) I said "thank you thank you thank you" to nurses and doctors and family members and friends and even strangers. When I wasn't in the hospital and interacted with "regular" people, I was nicer to them too. I went slowly through my day and thought I was the luckiest girl in the world when I got to make a trip to Walmart or Hyvee. And if someone was wearing a scarf or a woman happened to be sporting a shaved head out in public, watch out! I was your new best friend. We suffered from a similar disease and my empathy and compassion could not be restrained. I relished the time I had with my husband and kids in a way I struggle tapping into today. I spent lazy days hanging out with my mom and just enjoying our time together without trying to just get more done.

Number Two: The world was nicer. When you are bald and scrawny and sickly, people treat you better than when you are in shape and have a lot of hair. It's that simple. It's sort of embarrassing, but if I wanted some extra special treatment, I chose to wear a scarf instead of a wig. Strangers smiled at me when I was sick. They seemed inspired by the fact that I was buying groceries in their particular line and grabbed my hand and said things like "You have a very blessed day!" with enormous emotional sincerity. I am not ashamed to admit that I miss those days.

Number Three: It's extremely hard to live like you are dying when you're not. One would think that being saved from the precipice of death would be enough. It's not. At least for me (and I feel guilty about that sometimes, too). I am really just like everybody else now--which I guess bothers me. I feel like I should be producing more and changing the world since I just kicked cancer's butt. If I am not doing those things, what was the point of it all? Where's the redemption in the suffering? The truth is, many days I struggle with feeling unmotivated, overwhelmed, anxious, fearful, cynical, faithless, useless, unnecessary, disappointing and disappointed. Actually, saying all that out loud makes me sound like a big brat (add it to the list of failures ...).

Number Four: I had clarity. I knew exactly what I was supposed to do and I worked at it with all my heart: Get better. Take care of myself and myself alone. No one expected me to cook or clean or work. I had really solid excuses for anything I fell short on, and I used them with other people and with myself. I gave myself permission not to worry about anything. For having a potentially terminal disease, my level of peace and serenity was off the charts. I can't seem to get that back. I am realizing that I was able to trust God with my health and breath because I knew without a shadow of doubt that only He could save me. Somehow, since I have been "well," I have allowed myself to believe the lie that I have power to do everything else. Or that if I just work hard enough or worry long enough, I can somehow make everything in my life "work out" by my own power.

Clearly, this is some messed up thinking. Obviously, I don't want to have leukemia again. But talking this out reminds me that I worked really hard to keep my faith, my hope, my trust and serenity at the top of their game while I had cancer. And by "working hard" I mean praying with all my might. Trusting when there seemed to be nothing but bad news. Serving others and encouraging people even when I had every right to sulk in self-pity.

Reading, writing, and learning as much as I could about God's goodness and character and deep love and concern for my situation. Looking to spread love and support to those around me, as I went throughout my everyday life. I gave extra hugs and wrote thank you notes and spent time with people in ways that mattered. I told people I loved them. I was truly present when I was with people. My mind was not on a thousand other things I could or should be doing.

Because I don't have cancer now, these behaviors do not come as naturally as they did when I lived with a stronger possibility of death. However, they are not impossible to incorporate into my life today. Maybe having leukemia just primed the pump for the hard work that comes with living my ordinary, everyday life with the same extraordinary approach I had when I had cancer.

Night writer

I am writing at night. I NEVER write at night. I was sitting in my hot tub, trying to calm the crazy brain I have had today. All weekend actually. It's nothing bad, just too much. I couldn't keep my mind from racing so I tried the hot tub. It worked. Not the hot tub really, but the time alone allowed me to ask the question, "What could I possibly do that might help me get some peace of mind?" My solution, the one thing I do that always helps me live a little more like I desire to live my one and only life, is writing. So for better or for worse, here I go (I am confident that I will feel better--more relaxed and with better perspective--by the time I finish). Here's what I have been thinking about...

Thursday I had blood work done. I go in every three months and they test my blood to make sure it's all "normal" and there are no signs that my leukemia could be coming back. Usually, I don't give this a second thought. I assume I am cured. But recently, two of my leukemia friends have had theirs come back. I sort of got this stuck in my head Thursday and was an anxious mess. So I asked my doctor for some reassurance that mine was most definitely killed and my chances of it coming back were very slim. Bless his heart ... He was no help at all. He reminded me that for the first four years or so the chances are 50/50. Perfect. My heart started racing and I felt anxious and fearful off and on for the rest of the day. I was reminded of when I used to get my blood drawn every single day, sometimes more than once. When I wasn't in the hospital, I went every three days and had several transfusions. I lived depending on the results of those tests for five solid months. And at the end of that time they told me to come see them in THREE MONTHS for blood work. I remember begging them to let me come in at least every week. I had a hard time relaxing during the time between the tests. There was peace in being able to know daily that I was either OK or NOT OK. I could respond accordingly if I just had that information.

Lately, I have been relating this to checking my kids' grades online. I hate to do it every day (just like it wasn't enjoyable to give blood everyday), but it's way easier than waiting a couple weeks and then being terrified to check what has been happening to their grades the past two weeks. Sometimes we realize they forgot to turn something in or the teacher misplaced a paper or that their teacher clearly hated them and gave them a zero for no reason at all. But the main problem is, it's been too long and now they can't do anything about it. So, even though I hate checking every day, it's much less fear-inducing and productive than waiting a few weeks between logins. The damage is done by then and the anxiety of not knowing is greater than knowing the truth.

So, all that was helpful to get off my chest. But, alas, I do have a small point to make: when I take time to reflect on myself (my resentments, my failures, my shortcomings, my harsh words, my selfish acts, my bad habits, my signature sins) regularly, it's actually much less scary than when I put it off until one of those areas becomes a huge, serious problem. One that may or may not be fixable. It's not complicated; addressing areas of concern daily = little bitty fear. Addressing areas of concern monthly, yearly or perhaps never = massive, paralyzing fear. It applies to a lot of areas if you think about it; weighing yourself everyday is sometimes discouraging, but it's downright depressing when we wait several months and realize we have gained 10 lbs! And losing 10 lbs is obviously harder than cutting back for a couple days and losing one or two when we see the scale numbers creeping up. It might be simple things you avoid like not going to the dentist regularly or balancing your checkbook. Or it could be more important things like spending time in daily prayer and mediation or taking time to go on dates with your spouse or spending consistent quality time with your kids. All of these things have a better ending for us if we pay attention to them every day. And that's all I have to say about that. (Now you see why I never write at night ...)

"Treed"

The other night my cat jumped from my bed onto the top of my armoire. It stands a couple feet taller than me. I can't even begin to figure out how she did that (now, if you hate cats and cat stories, hang with me ... I have a good point at the end). The next day I was telling my husband about how cute she was just perched up there, sleeping and monitoring her little "kingdom" like the Lion King. He asked me, "So how did she get down?" I told him that of course she couldn't figure it out and I eventually had to lift her down. He said, "That's funny, seeing as cats are notorious for getting stuck in trees and unable to get down." You know, like in movies and in books where someone calls the fire department to get a kitten out of the tree for a frantic grandma/child? I'm not making any judgment statements, but just think about it--isn't that always the scene? Apparently, cats are really adept at getting themselves into dangerous situations but not so much when it comes to getting themselves out. Getting "unstuck." For that, they need outside help.

Me too. I can effortlessly "tree" myself. I can find myself in questionable or overwhelming circumstances that I got myself into all on my own--with very little thought or planning--and am powerless to reverse. Or worse yet, like a cat chasing a squirrel, I can run myself up a tree of obsessive or negative thinking and have no idea how to go back from where I came. Sometimes I arrived at these places because I wasn't paying attention to what matters to me. I was going along without a game plan and without boundaries. I wasn't keeping "first things first" and all that good stuff. A lot of the time, like with most cats that get trapped in trees, it's a result of fear. Especially when it has to do with what's going on in my head. I go places in my head that "it's not safe to go alone." Yeah, fear is a big one.

For a cat, and for me, there is only one solution to getting "unstuck": We gotta get some help from someone else. Sometimes it is enough for me to ask God. I pray, beg, bargain, and plead (like a Cubs Fan in the bottom of the 9th--game 7) for Him to save me: "Save me from my circumstances or help me survive them. Calm my brain and relieve my obsessive thinking. Help slow my thoughts and bring me back to sanity. Bring me back to realistic thinking, not fatalistic thinking."

God definitely has to be involved in the rescue plan. But more often than not, and this is the part I am really bad at, I need another human being. This is why people have sponsors and counsellors and mentors and wise friends around them. But there is only one design flaw to that plan of action: ***YOU have to make the call.***

Most people will not just happen along the street where you have been stranded in the tree for hours/days/weeks/months/years. You have to reach out and let someone know you need assistance. It's embarrassing to be stuck in a tree. So it makes it pretty hard to make the "ask." But I know I am at great risk of being trapped for a very long time and possibly hurting myself further if I refuse to admit I need help and reach out to someone else. It's hard because it makes me vulnerable. I don't want to appear weak or incapable of taking care of myself. But those are just ways that my giant ego prevents me from getting well. In order to come back to earth and not live my life huddled in the crevice of a tree (which, in case it hasn't dawned on you just yet, seems a bit more humiliating than asking for help), requires the loving words and listening ears of someone other than myself. And I have to say, it's much less of a spectacle to ask someone who loves me to assist in the getting "unstuck" process than having to call for the fire truck.

...On gratitude

The night before Thanksgiving I had the privilege of speaking for a few minutes at a Gratitude Meeting for people in all kinds of Recovery. Wall-to-wall people. Standing room only. They all came to hear and share how grateful they were for the good, the bad, and even the ugly that had happened in their lives. Because all of it led them to a Program and a God who rescued them from certain insanity and possibly death. I tweaked my talk a bit, but not much, for you to read. I talked about my two most personal diseases: leukemia and living with the effects of loving people who are addicted. Raise your hand if you or someone you know and love suffers from a life-threatening physical disease or the life-threatening disease of addiction ... That's what I thought ...

(So here's how it went ...)

Every day I read from a few books that all have dated entries. They are short and to the point and I love the fact that on those exact dates the author seems to be writing directly to me. I give credit to a God who knows my every need and speaks to me in this way. I anticipate what He will tell me each time I open to that exact entry. Last week I have to tell you that I was especially disappointed in the entry for a specific date. I felt like it was clearly written for someone else and was truly un-relatable. I considered that maybe God didn't pay any attention to my life at all. This is what the first paragraph said: "This is a time of abundance in your life. Your cup runneth over with blessings. After plodding uphill for many weeks, you are now traipsing through lush meadows drenched in warm sunshine. I want you to enjoy to the full this time of ease and refreshment."[22] I know ... right? This didn't describe my current situation at all. Things were hard and unknown and unstable.

I was paralyzed with fear and doubts and lack of faith at every turn. And THIS is what God is supposedly saying to me? Clearly, as we sometimes say in our home, "His cheese has slipped off his cracker." But after a day of thinking about how much this did not apply to me, as usual I calmed down enough to sit and ask God why He would dare say such a thing to me? And then He answered, "It's not your circumstances that determine if you live with a sense of your cup overflowing with blessings. Or, whether you feel you are traipsing through lush meadows vs. submerged in a pit full of mud. It's your perspective on them."[18]

Whenever we approach Thanksgiving, many of us reflect on the people and things in our life that we are grateful for. With a little effort, we can all come up with a small handful of blessings: our families, our pets, our jobs, our freedom, our health. But this year I have to say that I am especially grateful for two things that may or may not be found on most people's short-list: alcoholism and leukemia. I have had the burden and the privilege of learning how to do life while battling these two diseases. I used to roll my eyes at people who would talk about being grateful for the disease of alcoholism.

At the time I didn't understand that it wasn't the disease they were grateful for, it was for what the disease "triggered." They were grateful for the blessings and opportunities that the disease brought them. I get it now. Today, I feel that way too. There have been growth and wonder and power and miracles that I could have experienced in no other way.

There is nothing like learning to understand the maladies of a disease of the mind than by battling a disease of the body. Smack dab in the middle of fighting the disease of addiction, I was ambushed with the disease of leukemia. Both diseases have no rhyme or reason as to why one person is affected while someone else, who is possibly taking even less care of themselves, gets to bob along carefree and happy. Both diseases require outside help from people who understand the disease, if there is to be a fighting chance of healing and recovery.

I am happy to report that God and I kicked leukemia in the butt. I am currently in remission. Many of you may also be in remission from the effects and the constant threats of the disease of addiction. But there is one difference between remission from these two diseases that makes me especially grateful today: COMMUNITY.

When I had leukemia, I longed for connection with others who had the same disease as me. It gave me hope and camaraderie with people I had never met and had very little in common with. We knew that we both had a disease that could take our lives and that "shared affliction" bonded us in a way that no one else could begin to touch. In theory. I am done with leukemia. I get blood work every three months and sometimes visit my doctors or nurses at the hospital or give back by spending time with a newly diagnosed leukemia patient. Other than that, I'm on my own. I fought the good fight with the help of many friends and family and professionals and even strangers. But it's weird; no one really wants to continue to sit around talking about leukemia and the effects of the disease! Go figure. And the connection with other fellow sufferers is slowly fading into the busyness of real life. They have moved on and I suppose I should too.

But it's not like that in 12-Step Recovery Programs, what we call our "Fellowship." We don't just give you your discharge papers and send you home to go back to your "normal" life and muddle through your recovery on your own. We get to come together as often as we want and check in on how we are adjusting to or struggling with the challenges that come from living in remission. We remind ourselves that without this time of checking in with others who share a common affliction, our hope of lasting remission is slim. Emotional, physical, and spiritual relapse is just a matter of time unless we take care of ourselves daily through our readings and talking to others in the Program to give and receive support.

And just an observation regarding treatment for cancer: each type has a specific chemo regimen that can lead to recovery if it is followed. But that's where the diseases part ways. One of my favorite truths of this Program is that regardless of the particular brand of the disease we suffer from, the solution NEVER changes. We all have to work the same 12 steps if we want to be healed. We have to turn it all over to God. We have to let go of our resentments. We have to love and serve others and get our ego out of the way. We have to live every minute fully surrendered to God's will for our lives. It's beautifully simple.

I guess I am now one of "those" people who are grateful for their disease. As much as I don't want to return to living in the throes of the battle of addiction or of leukemia, I also am keenly aware and divinely reminded that their entrance into my life triggered the growth of the person I am becoming--a girl who trusts and loves and uses her brokenness to help other broken people. Someone who is free from the opinions of others and who strives to surrender her will to a power greater than herself. Someone who suspends judgment and reminds herself that everyone has a story and deserves to be treated with dignity. Someone who lives one day at a time and has tools to tackle the anxiety and the need to control that once dominated her. A woman who is learning to be grateful for every single part of her life because she believes God can use it all for good if she lets Him. As a result of my diseases, that I once considered *curses*, I am learning to become the kind of girl I never thought I could be. And I am learning to like her very much.

24

I'm really not sure where I am going with this. All I know is that it means *something* and I'll figure it out as I go. Ten days ago I drove my little self to Kirksville, MO to visit two friends that I went to college with. We met in 1989 (yes, I am old) when we were 18 and moved on with our lives in 1992. We didn't see each other again until last weekend.

The anticipation of that is hard to wrap your brain around. I wasn't nervous. I was excited but also curious as to how this was going to all pan out. Twenty-four years is a long time. Would we even have anything to talk about? Would we share the common chemistry that drew us together when we were practically children? Well, after our initial reunion, after we hugged and hugged and hugged some more, we didn't stop talking for the next 16 hours. Then we took a small nap, woke up and started again until we had to depart that morning. It was beautiful. It was like we had been sleeping across the hall from each other last week. There was an intimacy that has been hard to find since that time. It was like coming home to my family who knows me at my core, even when life has battered and bruised many parts of me.

I have many, *many* good friends today. But here's why I think it has taken me 24 years to develop those friendships and it took me only four to establish relationships that are solid enough to survive a 24-year gap--FORCED COMMUNITY. Today, for example, I don't feel well and am kind of emotional about some things, but guess what I am doing (besides writing--which is not that normal)? I am sitting on my couch, by myself. I am not calling my friend, who can't answer because she is at work, or another friend who has little kids she is picking up at school.

It's no one's fault. Life is busy and crazy. Neediness never comes at convenient moments. I am "handling" it on my own. I have had nights when I cried silently and privately so as not to upset my kids. I dried the tears and sucked it up. Occasionally I will call a friend and tell her what a hard night I had the night before or how angry or hurt I was a few days ago. But there's something less vulnerable and binding about doing it after the fact. It's entirely different to be melting down and have your roommate walk in from a date to find you in this pathetic state.

You can't cover it up or act tough. You are busted. You talk. You vent. You share. You are real and open in a way that comes naturally when someone arrives on the scene of your breaking point. Maybe you are different. More mature, or humble, than me. But being vulnerable at that level is very far out of my personal comfort zone. And when I don't live on a floor with a bunch of girls who might happen to "catch" me being broken, I don't usually feel the urge to announce it to anyone. This keeps me isolated and lonelier than I need to be. (This very topic is causing me to practically break out in hives). It's not that I don't have friends I can share with; I just have to choose to be open enough to do it.

And then there is the *reputation* thing. Image management. I want people to think I am together and mature and spiritual and productive. If I don't tell them about the ugly parts, they don't have to know them. It's much easier to pretend everything is "fine" when they only see you at lunch once or twice a month. There's also the *identity* thing. Somewhere between being adventurous and open-minded and in search of who I really was during college, I landed my identity in being a good mom and a good wife. Those are good things to be but they don't define me. I forgot to search out music I liked besides kid's songs and movies I loved outside of *Veggie Tales* and Disney movies. It's much easier to lose sight of who I am when I isolate. I forget that I am responsible to continue to not only take care of my kids and my husband, but to take care of *me*. To know what I like and don't like. It's hard to connect with others intimately if you are unsure of who you are.

I'm really not intending to sound whiney or as though I don't like myself or my life today. I absolutely do. But last weekend I was reminded that if I want the kind of relationships that stand the test of time, I am going to have to put myself out there a bit more than I do. We can never replicate the intensity that comes from living across the hall from our friends like we did in college, but an effort to let others in to our pain, our crisis, our chaos **as it is happening** is bound to expedite the process of securing the kind of friendships we long to have as adults.

Sigh ... I hate it when I give myself a good butt-kicking ... (gonna go phone a friend).

Party pontifications

Good news! I did it. I left the party early. I know I shouldn't have been there in the first place. That was my first mistake. But my guard was down and I just bounded into the room without thinking. It wasn't long before I realized I was headed for a day filled with regret if I didn't leave soon. Besides, it wasn't all that exciting, me being the only guest and all ... Pity-Parties are like that ... lonely and lame. Filled with thoughts and words that I later wish I could un-think and un-hear. But like I said, this time I did it differently. I showed up ready and rarin' to let loose as usual, but before I got caught up in the frenzy of emotions that are the trademark of any solid Pity-Party, I made myself pause and pray before I proceeded. Now I am happy to say that I have moved on with my day, free from the aftermath and emotional hangover that comes when I "party" too hard and stay too late.

Here's how I got to the party in the first place (and this is just one example of a hundred other times I have been previously lured in … see if it sounds familiar to you): I came across a book I got from a dear friend almost a whole year ago. In fact, when I cracked the cover I discovered an unopened Christmas card from her (sorry, friend!). The book, *Bread and Wine*, has an attractive cover so it has been displayed in my living room. It was written by one of my favorite authors of all time, Shauna Niequist, a woman younger than me who writes like I wish I could (... I start feeling the beginnings of what might be jealousy).

I open the book to accolades from other authors and see that they are from some of the best authors in their field. People I read and adore and revere (that feeling starts to grow bigger). I turn a couple pages and read her Introduction explaining why she wrote this book and why it is so close to her heart. That's when I am reminded why it's taken me a year to even open to page one. She is a phenomenal writer--smart, witty, poignant (which causes my jealously meter to rise a few more degrees).

But she is also touching on issues that I would rather not talk about. She expresses how much she loves to have dinner parties and share good bread, food, and wine around the table. This pushes me over the edge. How the heck does someone whose family is struck with the disease of alcoholism get to enjoy this book? Why should I even bother reading it? It is making me mad, quite frankly. Mad and filled with self-pity. Because now I am comparing myself and my life on several different levels and I feel like I am holding the short end of the stick.

Actually, I am feeling like I am stuck holding a prickly, dirty branch and SHE is holding a golden, magic wand. I have a conversation (one-sided, though it may be) with God that goes something like this, "Why can't I write like that? Why does she get to have famous writers sing her praises? How come she didn't have to even have cancer to be able to write something that matters? Why doesn't she have to deal with addiction and gets to have dinner parties with wine? Why can't my life look more like hers?" And I am even pretty certain that the bread and wine she keeps talking about isn't even going to her hips or belly like it does on most humans. "Why does God seem to love her so much more than He loves me?"

This is where the sanity-check comes in. When I stopped the insanity long enough to listen to my thoughts and to feel the emotions rising in me, I realized that I had a choice. And I chose to leave the Party early. A wise woman named Kay Warren teaches on this important concept of self-pity. She calls it the WITTY Principal: **W**hat **I**s **T**hat **T**o **Y**ou?[23] It's based on a teaching of Jesus' that goes something like this: A man agreed to be paid a specific wage for a day's work. When he found out another man had been paid the same wage for half a day's work, he argued with his employer. The employer logically addressed this by asking him, "Didn't you agree to work for that price for a whole day? Then why are you worried about how much I pay someone else? How is that any of your business?"

Everything in us screams, "But that's not fair!" As another wise woman I know always replies to that complaint, "FAIR is where you go to get a corndog." Life is NOT fair. But some other things that are not fair are OK with me. I get to live in America and not Haiti. That's not really "fair." Leukemia didn't kill me. That's not really "fair" either. My kids don't have disabilities or chronic pain or trouble making friends. Also not "fair." There are many, many people who would look at my life and feel like they are holding the short stick in comparison.

As usual, my daily reading coincided nicely, and divinely, with my little episode this morning. It talked about focusing on what I DO have rather than what I DON'T. Not on what I wish I had that someone else seems to have already secured. Here are two of the ending quotes: "If I can't recognize the love (also read: gifts or blessings) that *already* exists in my life, would I really appreciate receiving more? Let me acknowledge what has already been given to me,"[24] and "If the only prayer you said your whole life was 'thank you,' that would suffice."[25] -Meister Eckhart

So there you have it. An embarrassing but triumphant story of escape from an enticing but pathetic party. Perhaps someday I'll hit delete before I even open the invite, but for now, I choose to celebrate the small victory of early Pity-Party departure.

My miracle

Maybe I just need to get it out of me. Writing is so crazy to me. Mostly because I never wanted to write or liked it or felt remotely good at it. But now, when I write, I feel like I am doing what I am supposed to be doing. When I get too busy to write, doing other things, I don't feel peace about any of it. Instead of trying to squeeze it in to what I am doing the rest of my day, I need to make it a first priority and then everything else falls into place. And let's face it, the things that keep me from writing are not really actual jobs that need to be done; most of the time I am just stewing or fretting over what else needs to be done. Not the same thing.

I knew a guy in college who just sat down one day and decided to play the piano. And he did it. He learned to play by ear and would even sing at the same time. He eventually became a worship pastor at a church. I have always wished that could be me. You hear about those things occasionally. Like the kid in my son's class in 8th grade who decided to try his hand at long jump. That year he won State. What the *what*? Why can't this happen to me? And then I realize, it sort of did.

The fact that I have written anything, let alone hundreds of "things," that anyone reads or comments on is nothing short of a miracle of that caliber. Seriously. Little ol' me saying anything worth listening to in a way that isn't a jumbled blog of lame observations and unclear explanations of how I find meaning out of everyday life situations is equivalent to becoming a musician or gold ribbon athlete practically overnight. And, I have to say, that even though I didn't ask for it or practice for years or get any formal training whatsoever, I still know in my "knower" that this is a good gift from a great God who expects me to use it for *His* glory. Not mine. Which is pretty lucky for me because most of my blogs are somewhat incriminating and often show off some of my most embarrassing character defects. But since it's not about me, I can be OK with that.

I have to admit to you that when I sat down to write today, I did it just for me. I am having a day of questioning myself. I feel inadequate in pretty much every area of my life. I am taking things personally that have nothing to do with me and am having trouble reining in my anxious and controlling thoughts. I feel frozen with fear and dread over ridiculous things that are light years away from worries like dying of leukemia. But nevertheless, they are haunting me.

Writing is an attempt to focus on something else. Something that God has chosen to give me as a gift, even if it doesn't last forever. Writing is an avenue for me to get my bearings. To recalibrate my mind and heart. To remind myself of what I believe and don't believe. Which thoughts are lies and which are true. I can't say that I am 100% better, but I definitely feel like the pressure valve has been released and the sensation of being wound up and worked up and tensed up is slowly leaking out of me.

So, I write for you. And, I guess, I write for me. And the miracle of it all is not lost on me ...

Shopping for jeans

Today is the first day of a new year. I am happy to say that in the past few years I have been able to overcome, whether it is intentional or not, the urge to create a list of "Resolutions" (read: "unreasonably high expectations for myself and others"). No judgment on anyone who chooses to do so. For me, it became a list of all the ways I had failed in the past year and created pressure to perform (with certain disappointment) in the upcoming year. The "list" was usually violated within the first couple days of January. I have done it differently the past few years because I have committed to a way of living that includes examining myself daily and making adjustments as needed. It also gives me grace when I fail and a chance to start my "year" over at any point throughout my day.

That being said--part of why I am writing about this topic today is because I almost didn't. I almost didn't write because I don't feel like I have all my ducks in a row. It's really uncomfortable to write when I don't feel successful in managing my own life or accomplishing all I wish I could. It feels hypocritical. But as I begin this new year, it occurs to me that I might never reach a place where my "ducks" aren't swimming aimlessly around the pond or submerged, bottoms up, head under the murky water.

I am doing the best I can, but as soon as I corral a couple ducklings, a couple more pop out of the group and swim away. It's an endless and exhausting task. I am realizing that if I make adjustments throughout my day, with God's help, I can handle life as it comes. One day at a time. It doesn't mean I don't have principles that I live by, or routines and habits I try to incorporate, I just accept that I am much more likely to become someone I respect and enjoy if I don't set myself up by creating lists of expectations that I will most certainly use to beat myself up.

The other day I bought two new pairs of jeans. I paid cash because I used my birthday money. My birthday was in September. I have been carrying the money around in my purse for four months. Why? Because I was waiting until I reached the perfect size and weight before I bought anything new, before I deserved to spend this money on myself. I am proud to announce that yes, I have achieved this goal. Well--I should explain: I haven't reached the perfect size and weight I desire to be, but I have reached the perfect size and weight for where I am today. Because where I am at today has to be enough, especially because you can only wear the same pair of jeans so many times a week. Eventually you have to take them off long enough to wash them!

I had been living as if I weren't allowed to look good or spend money on myself or participate in the fashion world because I wasn't "where I wanted to be." I do this in other areas too. Sometimes I live with a

"When-then" mentality and miss out on living in the "here and now."

"*When* I can get this bad habit/sin/character defect under control or defeated, *then* I will reach out to help others grow."

"*When* I stop screaming at my kids, *then* I will call another young parent to offer support."

"*When* I make more money, *then* I will give to my church/that charity/that cause."

"*When* I have my spiritual life in perfect working order, *then* I will share my experience, strength, and hope with someone who suffers."

"*When* I know the exact words to say to a sick/separated/broken friend, *then* I will call."

Please hear me: the "***when***" is not coming. And I hate to be the bearer of worse news, but if you feel you have "arrived" at the perfect state and are now able to be of service to others, you might be in the most dangerous place of all. Just when we think we have it all together, there is undoubtedly more that will be revealed if we are open to seeing it.

We are always growing, changing, morphing. We will never "arrive" this side of eternity. So get on with the business of reaching out, loving, serving, helping, writing, calling, sharing, supporting, teaching, and shopping for jeans. Who you are at this minute is exactly who you are meant to be. Your greatest failures, flaws, and hang-ups are the very things that give value to what you have to offer.

I can't stop this feeling ...

"Lord, help me! I feel many things today, which I guess is better than feeling nothing. Not sure. But looking at my list of emotions, I feel: dreading, fearful, anxious, worried, insecure, rejected, distrusting, suspicious, disturbed, overwhelmed, uncomfortable, hurt, lonely, defeated, bored, exhausted, depressed, sad, disappointed, disappointing, irritated, envious, preoccupied, weary, restless, frustrated, annoyed. That's a pretty big list for someone who struggles to identify her feelings or has a propensity for feeling nothing at all. What's going on in me?"

... And those are just the ones from a list I found on the Internet.

I also feel aimless. Useless. Insignificant (those came from my own list in my head). Like I am not doing what I am supposed to be doing. Real estate is my job and I love it, but I know that doesn't define me. I long to write but I get scared of writing just like I get scared in real estate. FEAR--living in the future and all the "what-ifs" can paralyze me in the present.

I fear and question whether I will run out of clients or houses and fail to make ends meet, the same way I fear and question whether I will run out of things to write about. Neither of those things can I do much about except live day by day, trusting God for the results. I can try to write and make sure my heart and mind are in the right place, but I can't force the right words or message to come.

I can't produce a buyer or a seller; I can only put myself in a position to be available and share my business with others. I see a pretty strong pattern of mistrust of God's plan and God's timing as well as a default setting of trying to control and manage the outcome of my actions. It makes me crazy that A+B does not always equal C. Just because I do my part does not guarantee that the outcome I want will manifest itself.

I also have an inkling that some of my emotions have to do with being self-absorbed and selfish. Most of the time I spend is on me and my stuff--*my* family, *my* house, *my* job (which is laughable in and of itself since none of it is ultimately MINE). It's one thing to shoot off an encouraging text to a friend or someone hurting, but setting up time to sit with them and hear their pain or celebrate with them requires self-sacrifice. To spend my time serving someone else, just because it's the good and helpful thing to do, is not something I do regularly. Most days, I get up and do only what I want to do. None of these things are bad, really: Exercising, cleaning, reading, working, attending a meeting. But they all have one focus--ME. My agenda runs the show.

So--I don't know if this is the solution or not--the thing to do to alleviate the oppression of all these emotions. They are quite heavy. Making it hard to put one foot in front of the other. But maybe--just maybe--it is a good place to start. Get outside myself. Remind myself that the daily activities are just a means to an end. God has put us all here to be His messengers of love, compassion, grace, and hope. Everything else I do is just an avenue to this destination. Francis Chan talks about living at "the pace of love." That's hard to do when I have my own agenda driving the bus.

In a nutshell: Pray for and serve others. Give my literal time to others. Notice others as I go through my daily routine. Hold that routine loosely. Trust that God's timing and God's plan are perfect. Relax. Live in gratitude for the good I have and the bad I don't have. If I can manage to do even a few of those, maybe I can get relief from, and possibly even root out, most of these 24 emotions that have hijacked me this morning.

Are all your cards on the table?

Several years ago my husband and I led a Small Group. For those of you who are part of a contemporary church, you probably already know what that is. If you aren't familiar with the concept, it's essentially a group of people that meet together on a regular basis and is, um, *small*. The idea is that you do life together, in community. You share meals, you know each other's kids, you study the Bible or a topic and, in theory, you put all your cards on the table with these people.

Actually, the last thing on that list, "putting all your cards on the table," is the ultimate goal. The other activities are important but are intended to be catalysts for trust and familiarity so the cards can eventually make their way out of the box. It's also the hardest, scariest part, and one at which, I admit with sadness and regret, we were inept. I don't want to speak for my husband, but as a leader, I was definitely not at my "bottom" yet. I wasn't openly broken enough. I still had many character defects that needed to be fed by believing that others thought well of me.

That means that if I wanted to maintain my good, nice, spiritual-girl reputation, I had to keep my sharing at a PG rating. Sometimes I went all PG-13 on people just to test the waters. I mean, if people panic or push back on that, certainly my R-rated feelings or fears would send them running for the hills. So I kept myself in check. Sharing enough to relate but only conceptually, not in reality. I used phrases like "I struggle with being patient with my toddlers," instead of saying, "I'm so freakin' tired and worn out that some days I wish I could just run away from home and just yesterday I screamed at my kids as I threw down two boxes of 24 ct. yogurt packets and they exploded all over my kitchen and living room and ceiling!" And that's a true confession, right there. So, even though the goal of a small group was to share our raw and exposed lives together, I prettied up my sharing to save face.

I will never forget sitting with one of the girls from my small group. We had never hung out one on one before and I remember asking her how her marriage was doing. After being in said small group with both her and her husband for several months, I was surprised when she said, "Actually, we are thinking of getting a divorce." And they did. Now, I am not blaming the group or myself for this. But I most definitely take responsibility for creating an environment where, as a leader, I failed to model what it was to be open and vulnerable with my real problems. In my own marriage. In my own dark thoughts. In my doubting heart and ugly feelings. I don't know if sharing those things, those secrets that I kept in order to be a "good example" for others and maintain a certain reputation, would have helped them or their marriage.

But I do know this: not sharing them harmed everyone. Including me. It contributed to me living in denial and duplicity and left no room for hope or inspiration should I ever have relief or progress in defeating such flaws. My battles remained my own. They kept me lonely and helped no one. As a result,

I lived in shame and fear of being found out (though I am sure, people around me suspected that I wasn't perfect...). I also left no room for God to use my crap and redeem it by giving courage, strength and hope to someone else who might need to know that they are not the only one.

My sister recommended a book to me by Glennon Doyle Melton called *Love Warrior.* Many of you have probably read it. I cannot get past this one paragraph. It convicts me to the core and reminds me that God's plan for me is to bring myself to the table. Not my "representative." Not someone who acts as a substitute for the real deal. Not someone who just plays the part. He can only work through the true, authentic, broken me. The actual me. Not someone who just "represents" me in a poised, well-versed manner. Glennon says this about her relationships with friends and people she has known for years: "We've spent our time together talking about everything but what matters. We've never brought to each other the heavy things we were meant to help each other carry. We've only introduced each other to our representatives, while our real selves tried to live life alone. We thought that was safer. We thought that this way our real selves wouldn't get hurt ... It becomes clear that we are all hurting anyway."[26]

I am not thrilled that some 15 years after my small group leadership career has ended, I can say that I have been through the ringer with pain and loss and grief and addictions and cancer, but I also can't say that I regret what God has done in me as a result. Like the Velveteen Rabbit and Pinocchio, I finally became REAL. Able to be ever-so-slightly vulnerable. On most days (when I am emotionally and spiritually aware and healthy), I care more about how my story can be used for good than what you think about me as a result of hearing it. I devote significant time and self-talk and prayer to reminding myself of how to bring the inside me to the outside (as Glennon puts it) and avoid sending a "representative" in my place. This is my "living amends"(proving you are sorry by living differently) for the years of trying to be "shiny" on the outside and withholding the "shattered" on the inside.

Lord, give us courage to be ourselves.

The "tuck-in"

Most of these thoughts occurred to me last night after I'd been asleep for an hour, so don't hold it against me if they end up sounding ridiculous. Here's how it went: One of my kids woke me because he couldn't sleep and wanted to be "tucked in." So, I sent him back to bed and lugged myself up and staggered to his bedroom. I tickled his back and prayed and laid my head down next to his for a few minutes. Then, still half asleep, I hauled myself back into bed and begged God to tuck ME in, to help ME get back to sleep. Before

I dozed off, I thought, "There has got to be a blog in this somewhere." It didn't take me long to review my history of "tucking-in."

My husband and I are notorious for "over-the-top tucking-in." What takes normal people about 5-10 minutes to do, would take us close to an hour by the time we read to, prayed with, laid by, tickled, listened to and made countless trips to retrieve whatever necessary items our kids had forgotten to bring to bed but without them could never even THINK of getting to sleep. Things like blankies, stuffed animals, pacifiers, water, and more water.

I love the bit by Jerry Seinfeld where he evaluates how the whole "tuck-in" process has gotten completely out of hand these days. He said, "You want to know what my bedtime story was? DARKNESS!" No books. No water. No tickling. Just lights out and door shut. End of discussion. My kids are teenagers now and most nights I still tuck them in. It looks a little different (as in, no more pacifiers or stuffed animals) but is still a significant part of the bedtime process in our home. I have to admit that just like when they were little, I sometimes try to sneak past their room lest I be summoned to do one of them a favor by turning off/on their light, taking their cup to the kitchen, removing the pesky cat, bringing them a phone charger or running downstairs to record a show they started five minutes ago.

So how does this information qualify for a blog? Well, primarily because when I evaluate my own attitude toward the "tuck-in," I have to be honest and tell you that there are times when my level of patience and positivity toward the whole process basically stinks. Some nights I just want it to be over so I can get to bed or have some time to myself.

For my kids, the "tuck-in" matters because it helps them feel safe. It gives them comfort and security. It is time for one-on-one connection and affirmation. It's a time to be embraced and be heard. Just for that time period, all my focus is solely on them. This, it occurred to me, is how my relationship with God is, or could be, every minute of every day. Not just when I lay down my head at night.

But lucky for me, God is never distracted or resentful that I need just "one more" hug, glass of water, moment, or one more "chance." He's never too tired to hear just one more story or to listen to me vent about my day or cry over someone who was mean to me. He never rolls His eyes when I call out from my bed for a bit more time with Him. He never tries to sneak past my bedroom door so He can do more important things. He lingers there. He actually likes it when I stall. He relishes the time with me. And with *you*. He is the ultimate "tucker-in-er." And like my kids, I hope I never get too old to be "tucked-in."

...On editing

My editor (OK--my mom) and I have been going through my past blogs preparing them for the book. It's been fun to re-read them, but I definitely saw a pattern. When you read them back-to-back-to-back, you notice things. One might notice that there is a common thread of my struggle with control, anxiety, worry, fear, and lack of faith. On some occasions, I even act like I might actually have an answer to the same questions I pose only seven entries later. I sound a bit unstable, truth be told. I guess someone could call me wishy-washy, but I don't think that's really the case. My core values don't fluctuate, but how I approach people and circumstances can be different from day to day. Because, and this is deep, *people* and *circumstances* ***change from day to day.***

There is never one right way to approach every situation (love is always a "given"). I think this is something I have learned about life and about myself over the past five or six years. Hard life seasons tend to teach us things we can learn in no other way. We live in gray areas most of the time. I love the author Jodi Picoult[25] for this very reason. Everything she writes points to this truth. It's always a matter of perspective.

In her book *My Sister's Keeper,* she shows this by breaking the overarching story down into chapters that give the reader insight into how each character is affected by or involved in the story. When you read the chapter from the mother's viewpoint, inside her head, you are positive that she is doing the right thing for everyone involved. Then, you read it from the mind of her 12-year-old daughter. Her thinking is completely different and also seems to make perfect sense. Then the dad comes along and gives his two cents' worth and he too seems to have some solutions or doubts that make what the mom and daughter think seem absurd! Again--the world is not simple. It's a mix of colors that blend together into a lovely shade of gray (and I don't mean the scandalous-novel type).

What I see in myself, as I review several hundred blogs, is that I am learning to live in the gray-ness with serenity. That does not mean I have no backbone or opinions or standards. Everyone just relax. What it means for me is that I have learned, or am learning, to hold my opinions loosely. My judgmental side has drastically shrunk (though still a battle for me on occasion). Through personal heartache and suffering and from walking through the same with others, I have come to understand that life is complicated. Until I have walked a day in someone else's shoes, I have no room to determine what is best for them. And as I said in an earlier blog, thank God Almighty that it is not my job to do so. It's His. My job is to love and support and encourage.

This morning I searched and searched for this quote by Plato (I knew I had underlined it in one of my many daily readings): "Time will change and even reverse many of your present opinions. Refrain, therefore, awhile from setting yourself up as a judge on the highest matters."[27] Many of my convictions (which is sometimes a spiritual-sounding word for judgments or personal preferences as to how others should behave), that I thought I believed to my very roots, have changed over the past few years. So, I hope and pray, when I write I make it clear that these are my thoughts for today. They reflect what life has thrown me recently. They could change this afternoon. So I try my best to keep one theme and one theme only going through anything I put on paper: **Love God. Love People (myself included).** What is it that they say? ***"Everything else is gravy."***

Even if He does not ...

This entry is unique because I am typing it after the fact. I wrote it out the other day. I had thoughts that needed to come out on paper and I didn't have access to a device. My thoughts came much faster than my hand was able to write, so please be gracious if it doesn't flow very smoothly. Hopefully, the heart of it will come through and help you in some way ...

Today, I burst into tears because when I went to pay for the yogurt I was buying, it ended up being $12 instead of 2/$3 like I thought. Earlier that morning my garage door broke and I took it in stride. A real estate deal has potential to fall through after months of working on it and I was trusting God to help it work out as it should. But apparently, it's the yogurt that was the straw that broke the camel's back. This has happened often enough in my life that I have learned to pause and try to trace back my violent over-the-top reaction to its roots.

I think I am turning things over selectively. Only those situations I know without a doubt I cannot control. But selecting the yogurt that's on sale is something I should be able to handle. And on another bratty note--why can't I just catch a break? Don't I deserve to have something go my way for a change? I mean, honestly, I'm working my tail off to turn my junk over to the care of God; can't I at least get my yogurt at a reasonable price?

I was starting to think that this was all about control. Typically, in the same way that "Jesus" is always the right answer in Sunday school, "control" is my go-to defect at the core of most of my problems. But actually, I think it's something more this time: Expectations. I have placed expectations on God for how He should respond (or reward) me for my choices and actions. "If I" do this, "then He" should (fill in the blank with something amazing/wonderful). "If I" surrender this real estate deal to His care, "then He" should make it end in a flawless sale process. "If I" devote 20 years of my life to vocational ministry, "then He" should protect my family from the betrayal that can come from the very people we serve. "If I" teach my kids and raise them in the way they should go, "then He" should make them go that way.

When I put demands and expectations on God and catch myself thinking this way, I remember a message I heard from a wise pastor several years ago. You probably know the basic story of "Daniel and the Lions' Den." Well, before King Darius threw Daniel to the lions for not bowing down to his gods, there was another king who also insisted that the people only worship the idols made of gold. And it seems like kings in that day had a fetish for throwing people into places for disobeying, because a few years earlier Shadrach, Meshach, and Abednego had a similar problem, only they were threatened with a fiery furnace.

They refused to bow to anyone or anything but God himself and told the king, "We do not need to defend ourselves before you in this matter. If we are thrown into the blazing furnace, the God we serve is able to save us from it, and he will rescue us from your hand, O king. BUT EVEN IF HE DOES NOT, we want you to know, O king, that we will not serve your gods or worship the image of gold you have set up" (Daniel 3:18). EVEN IF HE DOES NOT. Even if I don't sell that house. Even if the job ends and I lose all my friends. Even if my kids wander away from what I taught them. Even if I fast and pray and beg and devote my days to bringing my prayers before God and STILL don't receive the answer I want, "THY will be done" is always better than "MY will be done." I don't always know what's best for me and I certainly don't know what's best for someone else.

So, I still pray. And I often ask again and again and again for a specific answer. But I am learning to hold the outcome loosely, with a heart that trusts that God loves me and hears me and has a bigger, better and more pure plan than any request or expectation I send His way. Even when things don't turn out the way I wish they would or think they should, I will still bow to Him alone. I will trust that He has a plan that is broader than my sliver of understanding.

***And in case you don't know the rest of the story--Shadrach, Meshach, and Abednego were indeed rescued. They were thrown into the blazing furnace, rescued by an angel, and the "fire had not harmed their bodies, nor was a hair of their heads singed; their robes were not scorched and there was no smell of fire on them" (Daniel 3:27). The king was so impressed by their God that he gave up his "pit-throwing" ways and declared that from then on everyone should worship the God of Shad, Mesh and Abe, and anyone who said anything against them would be cut into pieces and their houses be turned into piles of rubble. Um ... I think he might have missed the point, but I guess ya gotta start somewhere!

...On cussing

A few years ago I agreed to meet with a person who wanted to come to my house and talk to me because they had some "concerns." They were a member of our church and I was the wife of the lead pastor. I did it because, at the time, I thought that's what a "good" pastor's wife should do. They came over and proceeded to share their concerns about the fact that they had heard from someone else that when asked how my day was going I told them that I "felt like shit." They said something like I wasn't being a godly example to others and some other words that I really didn't hear through my shock. Now that I am older and more, um, seasoned, I can think of many good responses to that conversation. But at the time, I tried to defend myself.

I told them that I was certain that wasn't even true because I have a problem with cussing. And by that I mean that I am incapable of doing it so that it sounds like a normal part of a sentence. It's more like a defect, really. I could barely even bring myself to type profanity. Any cursing I do is a one-word expletive reserved for occasions when I do things like back into my own car or ride terrifying roller coasters. To use it in casual conversation is not something I do.

I am not saying I am above anyone; I just don't do it. It doesn't sound natural and isn't a part of my language gift set. So I knew this wasn't a true story. I don't remember what the outcome was, other than they eventually left our church and that I still regret letting such a ridiculous conversation take place in my very own living room. Or I at least regret that I spent considerable energy trying to defend myself without having a conversation about what really matters is our heart. I don't think I was capable yet. I still believed the lie that "bad" words = "bad" me.

Because as far as I can tell, words are words are words. I have seen a T-shirt that says "I love Jesus, but I cuss a little." It's possible. I have heard a lot of spiritual-sounding talk come from people like the one above, but their hearts are clouded with judgment and self-righteousness. I have heard a lot of passionate talk on forgiveness from a person who now looks the other way when they see me. Pretends I don't exist. On the flip side, I have also heard language that some like to refer to as "colorful" come from people who serve and love and sacrifice for their friends and even strangers who are struggling. Who genuinely try to turn their will and their lives over to God all day, every day.

Man looks on the outside, but God sees our hearts. It's legalistic to think that saying "Dangit!!" is better than "Dammit!" if I do it with the same angst or rage in my heart. I am kidding myself if I think that God is fooled when I clean up my language but not my spirit. That's what Jesus was referring to when he called the Pharisees in the Bible "white-washed tombs." In other words, they looked squeaky clean on the outside, but on the inside they were full of death. They didn't cuss or chew or go with girls who do. But God was not impressed. He saw the darkness of their hearts and condemned them.

Most of you are familiar with the 10 Commandments (one or two of them anyway). But the one that instructs us not to use the Lord's name in vain is the only one that even comes close to addressing our potty mouths. Yes, that means we should try to avoid screaming His name when we stub our toe. But it's not because it offends Him. "In vain" means to use it as an "empty" word. It means that we use His name without even considering that He is the most awesome, magnificent, all-powerful and loving and intimate Being in the universe. When we throw His name around willy-nilly (i.e. Ohmygod!), we are certainly not embracing the fullness of His name.

When my son was little, he heard about Hell in a Sunday school class. I guess he decided that it must not be a "bad" word since they use it in church. Not sure where he made the connection, but there was a period of time when he was about four that he would say things like, "What the hell just happened there?" to his grandparent, or "Ah, hell!" when he was frustrated. I was petrified that some Sunday he would yell out the door of his classroom at church, "Hey Mom! Where the hell have you been?" On the hierarchy we have created in the curse world, hell is about a mid-range curse word. But that's the point, we have created those words and their weightiness. There is not a word in and of itself that is worse than any other. It's the intent and state of our hearts that makes it so.

*And if you go around telling people that Heather Carter endorses profanity, you might have missed my point. I'd be happy to meet with you in my living room to clarify ... ☺

Clogged

I just knew if I gave it some time, I would find a great opportunity to brag about how my husband and I fixed our disposal a couple of weeks ago. All by ourselves. You have to understand something to fully appreciate this victory: we are not handy. I cannot emphasize this enough. Our strongest skills are being able to procure reasonable and competent outside help for repairs such as this. But my handyman had just left my house about 20 minutes prior after fixing a fixture in my basement, so I decided I would defer to YouTube and see if I could fix the disposal on my own. Long story short--I took a lot of things apart and then left for a meeting. Blake came home, inspected my work, put those things back together and christened the pipes with a gallon of Drano ... Nothin'.

We both felt very defeated and dreaded the bill that would come from calling Roto-Rooter on a holiday weekend. Good times. I continued to clean up all the junk I had pulled out from underneath the sink while Blake went downstairs to watch sports. About 15 minutes later, I heard a strange gurgling sound. I ran to the sink and saw the nasty, food-laden water receding and flushing down the drain! I did a little happy dance and yelled down to my husband, "We did it! We actually fixed something ourselves!" Such a proud moment.

This scenario came to mind today when I did one of my readings, which is written using scripture as if God were talking directly to me. It said, "Let Me fill you with My joy and peace. They flow into you as you sit quietly in my presence, trusting Me in the depths of your being"[28] (Romans 5:13). Before I even got to the end of the second sentence, my mind stopped, hanging on the word "flow." I thought to myself, "I think I am clogged." (Which, as with any normal person, triggered the above scenario.) I am like the pipes in my sink. And like my sink, a large amount of crap is clogged somewhere down deep. It's not a simple fix like pulling out a spoon or dishcloth that has gotten lodged in the disposal. Some of the blockage might be new, but a lot of it has been building in my pipes for months or even years. It's good and wedged.

When I harbor resentments over what others have done or regrets over what I have done, they can block this "flow" of joy and peace that God promises. Notice how God says we are able to be filled with this type of serenity: through TRUSTING Him in the depths (the yonder bowels of our clogged pipes) of our being. So, in essence, and I hope this doesn't seem crass, God is our Drano. He is our solvent. A solvent is defined as "the liquid in which a solid is dissolved to form a solution." Isn't that perfect? We have clogged pipes. When we trust God and turn our will and our lives over to HIS control, He acts as a solvent to weaken and dispel those things that are preventing His peace and joy from flowing freely through us.

Even though I am coming to grips with the reality that my plumbing expertise was not the primary factor in relieving my clogged drains, I can say that my part was crucial to the process. And ultimately, SOMEONE had to go buy the Drano and pour it in. If we want joy and peace to flow freely in us, we have to turn to God and acknowledge that He alone has the power to unclog us. But, just like the Drano, it takes some time. It is not immediate. After I had done all I could with the drain, I moved on and started cleaning.

And while I was doing my work, the Drano was doing its work.

Maybe it seems like a stretch for you, but yesterday I was having trouble with this trust thing, so I tested this approach. When I felt overwhelmed and out of control and anxious, I would ask God to be my Drano. To dissolve the junk in me and open my heart. To take care of situations that I was powerless over. It was a good image for me to carry. But now I am faced with the hard truth; I didn't fix *anything*. It was the Drano all along.

The "Good and Lovely" Game

Something I am realizing as I get older is that it is quite possible that even though my skin is sagging and my hair is a bit more silver, my insides might always remain about 12. As in 12 years old. I remember being 20 and anticipating the day I turned 30. How I would finally arrive and have the wisdom of Billy Graham and the grace of Jackie Kennedy. I believed it wholeheartedly. Let's just say my 30th birthday was a little disappointing.

Now I am, um, much older than 30. And my insides are lagging far behind my outsides. So, my conclusion is that I might never grow out of some of my struggles with worry, control, self-consciousness, pride, or moodiness. However, the one thing I can say for my decades of battling with my mind and heart and will, is that the tools I have found to remedy those broken areas have indeed improved. Let me tell you about one of them I have found to battle an obsessive, worried brain. It's actually not something new I *learned*, it's just something I finally *tried*.

It started this summer (I'm a slow learner). I was awake in my bed, having rolling anger fantasies about a person. I certainly couldn't sleep for all the obsessing going on about what they had done and how it had affected me. My mind was like a tornado--chaotic and powerful and deadly. And then the "Heather version" of a scripture came peeking around the corner of the crazy: "Whatever is good, whatever is lovely, think about these things."

I knew there was more to the verse than that, but this was all I could do from memory. So I tried it. We had been at the fair all day so that was fresh in my mind. I distinctly remember thinking, "Baby pigs are good and lovely. Horses are good and lovely. Funnel cakes are good and lovely. Lemon shake-ups are good and lovely. Fried candy bars are good and lovely."

And so on and so forth. When I ran out of gratitude for components at the fair, I switched to things I could see around me. "My bed is good and lovely. My car, my yard, my hot tub, my kids, my cats, are all very good and lovely." This went on for a long time, until my mind could come in for a landing and let me fall asleep.

This past week I have awakened in the night on a few different days, panicky and overwhelmed with everything I have to do the next day or about ways I have fallen short the day before. My fear and anxiety over all the people I can't control (specifically, my kids: their friends, their grades, their jobs, their money management, whether they know how much I love them, whether I have damaged them in ways they will blame me for later on, whether I am tough enough or too lenient) and situations I am trying to manage (in real estate, in my writing, in my ambitions). Whether I have a teensy bit of power to do anything about these areas is questionable but doing anything about it from my bed at 2:00 a.m. is not. I know my limitations. I'm not a complete idiot.

This morning, after a night of playing the "Good and Lovely" game, I decided to look up the actual verse. It's from Philippians 4:8. A guy named Paul is encouraging people to keep their minds right. The entire verse goes like this: "Whatever is true, whatever is noble, whatever is right, whatever is pure, whatever is lovely, whatever is admirable--if anything is excellent or praiseworthy--think about such things."

I didn't even remember until I read the previous part of the passage that these instructions were given as the solution to a problem: they were battling their anxiety. Well, what do you know? I am not the only one.

People have struggled with this for thousands of years. Paul says, "Do not be anxious about anything, but by prayer and petition, with thanksgiving, present your requests to God. And God's unfathomable peace will follow." I am just about done (though I still try really hard, occasionally) lamenting my tendency to become a hot mess of worry and fear and anxiety. But there are solutions if I choose to implement them. And in my case, I will continue to work on mastering the "Good and Lovely" game as if I were preparing for the Olympics.

Emergencies

The other day, as we were headed out the door for school, my daughter remembered that she needed shorts for her PE class. Black shorts and only black shorts. It was a Monday morning, so our weekend laundry piles were still teetering on the dryer in the basement. We searched and searched like maniacs for a few minutes, but she ultimately had to settle on some shorts that were actually mine (can you imagine anything worse as a teenager?). As we were running throughout the house, I mentioned, in a not-so-patient tone, that it would have been ideal if she had thought of this the night before rather than as we were walking out the door for school. Naturally, she was grateful for my astute insight.

As I sat in a study group a few days later, discussing different modes of prayer, I had a flashback to that Monday morning mania. Basically, the reality of the practice of prayer is often vague and open for much interpretation. And while there is no recipe for "right" praying, there are definitely some ways to go about it that will benefit us and God differently. And thinking about the emergency of the misplaced shorts, I can see some similar issues related to prayer.

Is it wrong that my daughter couldn't find her shorts and had to search frantically for them? Not really. Annoying? Yes. Stressful? Yes. Effective? Not so much. But we did find something she could use until we could look for her own shorts after school, when we had more time.

Regarding prayer: is it *wrong* that we throw out emergency one-liners to God? Does He still listen? Does He still answer? Here's what I believe about it: No. It's certainly not wrong when we do it and Yes, He hears and answers. However, there is something to be said for the daily-ness of it. How would our life look different if we were intentional with God on a regular basis? And by "regular" I mean as often as we can every moment of the day. If we put our clothes away as we folded them so they could be easily located when needed *and* we prepared ahead of time what we needed to take to school in the morning?

Get it? Less stress and chaos. Same with prayer. Maybe if we were intentional about the minute-by-minute, hour-by-hour time that we talk with God and listen back, our emergency prayers would be less necessary. Because we wouldn't create our own emergencies by ignoring our "laundry" that has been building and building. If we can maintain a constant, steady stream of conversational prayer and times of leaning into his still small voice, we may not need to throw out those cries for help about what to do and how to do it. At least not as often or as a result of neglecting to be in regular communication with Him. If we daily align our will with God's through His word and meditation and surrender, the answers that used to stump us will be a natural part of who we are, what we want, and how we think. The "desires of our heart" will match up with His.

So once in a while, it's OK to forget about your PE shorts until the last minute. But if that becomes a habit, it might be time to slow down and think ahead and maybe keep on top of that pile of clothes that threatens to create a black-shorts emergency. In spiritual terms, praying without ceasing will put you in a position to hear and be heard by God. The serenity that comes with that way of life is what makes His yoke easy and His burden light.

I want my way!

I am a Realtor. When people ask me how I like being a Realtor, my response is, "I love it!" That's mostly true. I have to be honest and tell you that I have noticed that I love it most when deals are going *my way*. In my favor. When everyone agrees on a reasonable price and reasonable repairs. When there are no surprises and my listings sell quickly and the sellers are happy with me. When we find the perfect house in record time and the sellers and buyers can come to the closing and are nice to each other. When all of those factors are present, I really do "love" my job.

But here is a little secret in real estate--and possibly in your job and maybe even the remainder of your life in general--things don't always go this way. In fact, it's rare that any "deal" that involves breathing people will ever move along flawlessly. We all bring so much to the table. It takes a lot of sorting and shuffling and managing the baggage to get anything done at all. It's really a miracle any of us can collaborate and negotiate to come to any conclusion that is beneficial. We all carry so much fear about not getting what we want and about losing what we have (whether it's stuff or control or power or security or even love) that it can quickly rise to the surface in some not-so-pleasant ways.

But I digress, because my real reason for writing all this down is that I am struggling. I am struggling to live in the truth that I know, which is, "Things aren't necessarily going bad just because they aren't going *my way.*" So I need to reason this out on paper, with you, to hash out the irrational fears that cause me to "not love" my job and my life in general.

Does anyone else ever get trapped in this type of thinking? We have desires and goals for ourselves and our marriage and our fitness and our parenting and sometimes we even set some pretty nice goals for other people (which they don't even seem to appreciate or intend to work toward!), yet nothing seems to be going the way we planned. Or worse yet, the way we *prayed*. We are working our hardest for the end result and it all seems to be going in the opposite direction. It doesn't look anything like we pictured it or expect it to look if God actually loved us. We are convinced our life is horrible and God has not heard us or is maliciously withholding good things from us. Maybe that's just me.

I guess it comes down to this: I don't always get *my* way (luckily) because *His* way is better and bigger than MY way. Don't get me wrong, I really like it when I get my way, and my husband and parents will tell you that I am pretty good at getting it. But I can also think of many, many times when, if I had actually gotten what I thought I really, really wanted, I would have been in deep weeds. The outcome would have been disastrous and heartbreaking. It's also important for me to remember that my happiness is not always the only priority in the situation. Go figure.

Sometimes if a house is not selling when I want it to, it's because God is bringing that exact home to the exact right person exactly when they can afford to buy it. Sometimes He doesn't lift all the pressures of mean friends off my kids because He is teaching them something about forgiveness and compassion and trust.

Sometimes I can only reach the goals I have for myself by learning through the challenges and frustrations that come with conflict and opposition. Sometimes my limited vision and knowledge of my circumstances causes me to doubt the reality that *my* world is not *the* world.

There are bigger things at stake for people around me that require things to not always go my way. Right now feels like a good time to interject a juvenile "DUH." Maybe you are all way ahead of me in this area. I pray that is true. But in case you occasionally question why you are having such a "bad" day, month, year, maybe you can try to remember these truths with me and …

TRUST IN THE LORD WITH ALL OF YOUR HEART AND LEAN NOT ON YOUR OWN UNDERSTANDING. IN ALL YOUR WAYS, ACKNOWLEDGE HIM, AND HE WILL DIRECT YOUR PATHS. (Proverbs 3:5)

God's path tends to look very different from the one we have mapped out for ourselves (and passed on to Him for approval). But if we practice trusting that He has a plan and we are a part of it, we will be able to relax and take it in stride when things don't seem to be going our way. We will eventually build a track record of trust, knowing God's way is always the best way.

(There. I think I have sufficiently talked myself off the ledge for now. Thanks for your help!)

I see those hands ...

Raise your hand if you have ever battled a potentially terminal disease or love someone who has or does. Now raise your hand if you struggle with the disease of addiction or love someone who has or does. And raise a hand if you've ever felt tormented by the effects of your own sin/evil/brokenness or have suffered from the effects of living in a world riddled with the effects of other people's propensity toward sin/evil/brokenness. Anyone running out of hands?

Today I awoke with a fresh fervor for why I started writing and why I keep writing. I started writing because I had cancer. I keep writing because through cancer, and through throwing out my life on "paper," I have learned a few things. I have come to believe through a combination of reading and listening and experiencing that most humans (at least in the world I operate in here in America) have three common strands woven into the fabric of their life experience: Disease (of the body and the soul), Drugs (and by this I refer to anything done addictively), and Deity (the pursuit of and issues with God).

I think we would be hard-pressed to find an individual who has not spent significant time enmeshed in these overarching areas. I used to think that the majority of the awfulness of a disease or an addiction was reserved for the patient or person harboring it. Not so. I have watched my family suffer great sorrow and consequences from my leukemia. And I have been profoundly affected by the addiction of people I love, in ways that impact the way I behave in every other part of my tiny sphere of influence.

We talk about the God stuff (Deity) every time I write--but let's take a few minutes to focus on the other two. Disease and Drugs. Just to prove my point about how often these two deadly animals rear their ugly heads, let's talk about movies. I didn't notice it so much until these areas were acute in my world. When I was in the hospital for six days at a time getting chemo, I watched a lot of movies. Almost without exception, at some point in the movie, one of the characters would deal with cancer or alcoholism/addiction. Even if I had seen the movie before and hadn't recalled that being a theme, one of them would inevitably be mentioned or dealt with.

I remember renting a movie about a young woman's battle with early onset Alzheimer's. That seemed safe to me. But no. Her father's alcoholism came into play, eventually. I think you would be hard-pressed to find a movie that doesn't address these two awful diseases, either living with them or dealing with the aftermath of them. And why is this? Because these particular struggles hit the heart of almost every movie-goer. Almost every person we know.

Because Disease and Addiction are so rampant, I believe it is not a stretch at all to say that every person has been affected by one or the other sometime in their life. Even if it isn't active, the coping mechanisms one develops to deal with someone else's Disease/Addiction are often carried on generation after generation. And many of these skills we carry are not healthy or good for us or those we are in relationships with. Often those *affected* by the diseases are even sicker than the carrier. They can be angry, bitter, self-righteous, co-dependent, pessimistic, judgmental, etc.

I guess my point in it all is that whether it's our own personal battle or we are suffering from the "secondhand smoke" of Disease/Addiction, there is much shrapnel still embedded in us and it affects how we behave. And we need to realize this about others and how they behave. We are all doing the best we can, but to some degree we are all 'sick." Extending compassion, understanding, and empathy for our fellows is crucial. Extra kindness and gentleness are required for survival and healing for all of us. How people behave usually has less to do with us and more to do with what that are going through and have been through. Therefore, be gracious to one another.

Try your best not to take it personally. Treat your brothers and sisters like you would a "sick" friend.

Because we all are.

Embrace the madness

March Madness. In our house it's almost considered a holiday. When my husband Blake was in college, he would actually grow his hair out all year and ceremoniously shave it the day March Madness began (I am speaking of a month-long frenzy of college basketball play-offs, in case you are not the sporty type or are not living with someone who is). Part of the "Madness" is obvious. Tons and tons and tons of games-all-month-long. I am convinced that there is also an unspoken (or possibly out-spoken) "Madness" that comes from family members of those who must watch all of these games.

I was trying to talk to Blake last night when I noticed he seemed a bit distracted (he was kind of dancing with his feet like a toddler who had waited too long to go to the bathroom). I asked him what was wrong and he just spouted, "March Madness." Games had started and his mind was already downstairs on the couch, soaking in the energy of the competition.

But over the years of being associated with someone obsessed with March Madness, I have joined in occasionally and listened to the pontifications of my husband regarding the whole experience. I have concluded that much of the "Madness" comes from the upsets. The team that was expected to win the whole tournament loses in the first round. Or a team that has never even made it to the tournament before rises and surprises. People are angry because their bracket is "destroyed in the first round" (and by "people" I mean the boys living in my house).

All this has got me thinking lately, primarily because I am sensing the "Madness" of my own life. I feel like I am a number 1 seed (OK, maybe more like a 3) for a good stretch of time and then inexplicably drop to the worst ranking possible. In sports lingo, I am in a "slump." Even though all the statistics point to a winning trajectory, I just can't pull it off. My slump affects my attitude and my motivation and my confidence. Things around me just seem to go in the opposite direction than I want them to go. If a situation has potential to go south, it seems to go there every time lately. It's become almost comical (in an infuriating and discouraging sort of way). So I looked up some info on "slumps" in the sports world, and realized the reasons and answers are pretty much the same with sports as they are with our lives.

The first thing sports psychologists tell us to do is to try to identify the root of the problem. One article said, "Many athletes are unaware of the causes of a slump, so they look in the wrong places for a solution. As a result, they fall even deeper into a slump." Sometimes we have to look at our lives and do a check. Are we still doing the basics? Are we eating right, exercising, reading, praying, sleeping enough, spending quality time with friends, making time for fun, keeping first things first? Have we been neglecting any of these areas? Much of the time I can see a lag in one or more of these areas. I need to tweak my game and get back to the basics. That can sometimes get me out of a slump.

But sometimes, those areas seem to be in working order. This is where it gets dangerous. This is when we start to blame outside sources. Our "teammates" if you will. Or stupid calls that the ref made. This is when we have to keep the focus on ourselves, since we are ultimately the only one we can do anything about. The slump will never end if we depend on what's outside of us to fix the inside of us.

A few other tips for managing a slump:

1) **Focus on the task at hand.** Don't get attached to the outcome. Just do the next right thing, one day at a time, and more than likely slump will heal itself. Sometimes we just can't figure it all out. We have to just keep moving forward and not quit. Remember that "this too shall pass."

2) **Don't compare.** Don't compare your insides with other people's outsides. Or even your outsides with their outsides. Comparing will lead to despair and frustration, ultimately prolonging your slump.

3) **Relax.** When you try to force a solution before its time, you can exacerbate the problem. Trying too hard in life, just like in sports, typically makes the problem worse. Keep your eyes on the big picture. Don't over-think or over-feel it. We don't know what God has planned for us or others. We are always a part of the plan. Trust that He will bring it to fulfillment in due time.

And the number one thing to remember when you are in a slump is that it's not personal. Slumps don't discriminate in sports and they don't discriminate in life. The rain falls on the just and the unjust. The sun shines on the evil and the upright. Even the best sports teams and athletes go through slumps in their careers. That's perfectly normal. It's part of the deal.

Keeping it simple (or Strawberry fruit snacks)

I was at the dentist yesterday. I have mentioned before how amazing my "dental spa" is. Besides having amazing attitudes about a not-so-fun job, they go the extra mile when dealing with a frightened child who has anxiety about having dental work done (and in this case, I am not talking about myself …). Apparently, the little boy in the station next to me was getting his teeth cleaned for the first time. Naturally, he was nervous about having all the tools stuck in his mouth.

The technician talking to him made it sound like he was preparing for a ride at Disneyland! When they got ready to polish his teeth, I could hear them list off his choices of flavors: Strawberry Fruit Snack, Orange Juice, Peppermint Candy Cane, Pink Bubblegum, or Vanilla Ice Cream. I mentioned to the girl getting ready to polish my teeth that A, I felt like I wanted to switch my choice based on those new descriptors and B, I also felt like they were setting that kid up for some major disappointment. Talk about "over-promise and under-deliver"! Maybe they should also mention that the Strawberry Fruit Snack will feel like it has been rolling around in the sandbox for a few days! There is no special flavor that will make up for that unpleasant mouthful of grit.

I guess I can appreciate their efforts when I really think about it. I mean, no one likes to go to the dentist, even for a mere clean and check. And let's face it, getting a filling or a root canal can be as pleasant as, well, getting a root canal. But we do it anyway if we want to keep our teeth. It's a no-brainer. We can either do the necessary deal with Novocain, laughing gas, anesthesia, song and dance and a plethora of flavored tooth polish, or we can do it without. Either way. It has to be done.

This is how I see life with God. Sometimes life is good. Very good. With blessings galore and shiny-happy people everywhere. At times like these, I find it easy to trust and love God. But there are other times that life just plain sucks. Times when we don't want to pray or smile or get out of our beds. Then what? God tells us that "in this world we will have trouble."

That's just how life works. And the temptation is to blame. Much of the time, people land on God. They decide He is not loving and that they are better off without Him. I mean, why even serve a God who just lets crap happen to us if He has the power to stop it? Why listen to or obey His rules if I still end up suffering just like those who ignore Him? Where's the reward? Where is the sense of blessing? Where are the feelings of happiness and peace that I am promised if I love Him?

These are questions I have asked. And there are others that are even more in-His-face than these. But here is the question I have to ask myself: "To whom shall I go?" I can either do this hard life with God or without God. The one who suffers most, if I choose to be angry or ignore Him, is me. Doing life on my own hurts me and those around me. It doesn't "stick it to God" when I choose to go off on my own. When I try to live by my own power and self-will, without the wisdom, discernment, guidance, strength, and hope that comes when I choose to trust Him. It's like going to the dentist. It's something that is inevitable. But we can do it the easy way or the hard way. With the tools and provisions to make a potentially painful experience better or without them. With a dentist who is kind and patient and understanding of our fears or without.

I know this may sound like I am oversimplifying things, but my tendency is to make things harder and more complicated than they need to be.

So, for now, I am going to go with *simple.*

Twisted Sister

A friend and I were throwing around ideas about titles for the book I am working on. I was wondering out loud how to concisely communicate that I am a messed up, broken, often immature girl with a lot to say ... hmmm. After a few ideas that might offend, she said, "How about *Twisted Sister*?" It may not win, but the idea is definitely worth writing about. It only took us a couple minutes to relate this to Jesus (nothin' like mentioning Jesus to silence a room ☺). I am not like Him in more ways than I can count, but I am like Him in a couple areas. We are both a little twisted. I don't mean to be disrespectful of Jesus. I don't mean to call Him psychotic or anything. He just approaches things with a "twist" that was unheard of in His day and age. My writings are not that earth-shattering, I realize. But I do see our "twisted-ness" relating in a couple ways:

1) We both like to twist/challenge the way people have always done it. Or thought it. He is sort of famous for using the phrase, "You have heard it said (fill in the blank with something like 'do not murder') but I say to you (fill in the answer with something like 'anyone who hates his brother has already murdered him in his heart')." He raised the bar and addressed the sins of the heart. The yucky stuff you can try to dress up and cover up but still lurks in the dark places of the soul. You might have read my blog "On cussing." That's exactly the kind of thing I am saying. And hopefully, what I say lines up with Jesus when, even as He is calling people on the carpet to live authentically, he also extends exorbitant amounts of grace and compassion.

2). We both interlace (or twist) truth and spiritual principles together with everyday life. Just look at all the parables that Jesus taught on. He used examples of people, places, or things around Him to make His point. He referred to scenarios that any person in His circle of influence would relate to. He shared how we should live by talking about a lost son, a lost coin, a lost sheep, a good citizen, a shrewd employee. I am pretty sure Jesus would have used squirrels (see my blog on "squirrels" on my site) to make His point if he saw one running around Galilee. I have written on topics such as blood, platelets, Neil Diamond, Seinfeld, and going to the dentist (that's hard to make interesting, right?). If we are looking, God and His spirit can be "twisted" into everything that happens in any given day.

So there. I am not afraid to admit it: I am one "Twisted Sister." But it seems I am in good company.

"Duh!"

I think I have mentioned before that I am a little slow on the uptake. Here's yet another example of a truth I have held onto over the years that isn't actually true. As a result, I have been frequently disappointed but, most embarrassingly, I am guilty of attempting to manipulate God into doing for me what He never promised to do. I didn't do it with a heart of selfishness or with dark motives. I truly thought I was trusting Him to give me the power to make it through the day.

My revelation was sudden. It reminds me of how they tell you when you are working out (if you don't work out, you'll just have to trust me on this) that if you just adjust your weights/body position about a quarter inch, it will greatly enhance your results. Just the tiniest bit is all it takes. And the slightest adjustment, a minuscule tweak, in how I view the following words God gives us, made all the difference in the world.

You may have heard and even tried to apply the following teaching from Philippians 4:13: "I can do all things through Him who gives me strength." Here is how I have abused that verse: I rack up a bunch of activities and stretch my life to a thin thread so that I am exhausted and emotionally strung out, and then ask God to give me His strength to survive it. It sounds a bit crazy when I lay it out like that, yet I have been practicing this strategy for years.

I read something recently that slapped me flat across the face on this approach. It's from a book called *Twenty-Four Hours A Day.* Regarding this very verse, the author says, "This does not mean that you are to do all things and then rely on God to find strength. It means that you are to do the things you believe God wants you to do and only then can you rely on His support of power."[29]

That never even dawned on me. Seriously. Can you say, "Heather. World."? (Picture the world literally revolving around my body as you read that.) I have elevated my plans and my agenda over God's plans and His agenda. Rarely do I follow another important instruction God gives which is to practice saying, "If it is God's will, I will live and do this or that." I just keep doing what I want and asking Him to bless it and give me the strength to carry it out. That's messed up.

It is tempting for me to excuse this ceaseless activity by pointing out--to myself--that most of my activities are good and helpful to people I care about and often even strangers. Wouldn't that all be part of God's divine plan for me? Surely He wants me to serve others on His behalf. We are to be His hands and feet, right? This is all true; however, if I look just a bit deeper and with an honest lens, I have to admit that much of it is ultimately image-management. It means that, at the root of it, I am mostly interested in what others will think of me. I want them to be impressed with how I can manage to live a frenzied life for Jesus, and how I appear to do it with grace and poise and loveliness (this is just getting worse all the time).

I think I will just stop now with the true confessions. But I most definitely am committing to pause, pray and proceed before I take off running like a wild woman, expecting God to sustain me in the madness.

Resentment machine

When I write a blog, it usually is a result of something I have read in the morning that I feel God is prompting me to write about. Most of the time it is a direct result of something I am battling with myself and you, my dear friends, get to be the victims of me "reasoning things out" on paper. But today, I want to share a few things that have been on my mind since I watched a movie last week. It was called *The Light Between Oceans*. It isn't necessary to recap the plot in order to help us reflect on a quote that I just can't quite get out of my mind. In part, I think it is because I am realizing that even though it sounds good and beautiful, it's missing a very important component that unfortunately, I have learned firsthand in the past several years.

A couple different characters use this eloquent reflection on forgiveness and why it is always the best choice over resentment. Let me tell you the quote and you see if you can find the flaw: "It [forgiveness instead of resentment] is so much less exhausting. You only have to forgive once. To resent, you have to do it all day, every day. You have to keep remembering all the bad things ... No ... we always have a choice. All of us."[30] I do have to say that I am very proud of this movie for posing this as the best solution. We so love movies that have an exciting revenge plot! Just "letting it go" is not that glamorous and seems pretty unfair. So, in that respect, kudos to Hollywood.

But here is what I have found in my challenge to forgive: There is no way in heck that it's a one-time job. Depending on the depth of the hurt or betrayal, choosing to forgive might be something I have to decide to do every single day for the rest of my life. And often, several times a day, at that. Is it just me? And I have to say that the choice to forgive has to be a selfish one. What I mean by that is that I do it for my own peace of mind and serenity. If I had to rely on my desire to do it for the person I need to forgive, I'd never get there. There is something miraculous that happens when I make the decision to "let it go" for my own sake. It becomes a habit and, over time, I might actually have some softer feelings to match.

Resentment, I agree, takes a lot of work to hold on to. And yes, clinging to it causes me to rehearse and re-rehearse the offense. I heard a speaker liken it to the sports announcers using the instant replay machine in a sporting event. Have you ever watched them review an injury on the football field? They play it over and over, in slow motion, and in the end it looks even worse than the first time it happened. That's how resentments work. And yes, they are exhausting. I love these lines in my *Courage to Change* book on Recovery: "When my thoughts are full of bitterness, fear, self-pity, and dreams of revenge, there is little room for love or for the quiet voice of guidance within me ... I know that when I hold on to resentment and blame, I occupy my spirit with bitterness."[31] I love the way they put that: "I occupy my spirit with bitterness." It is up to us to de-clutter our spirits from resentments so we can find more fulfilling and nurturing way to fill ourselves up.

So, I would just add an addendum to what the movie is trying to say regarding forgiveness. *Both* choices will most likely present themselves to your heart and mind on a regular basis. Every time you choose to resent, to replay that resentment machine over and over and over in your head, you will occupy your spirit with bitterness, and it will keep you captive--unhappy and angry and very, very, very tired (I know this from experience also). But even though forgiveness is not a one-and-done event, there is a wonderful thing that happens the more you do it. You become more and more free. You will be able to hear that still small voice of God that gets drowned out when resentment rules you. You will be lighter in body and spirit because each time you do it you will unload a little bit more of the baggage you have been hauling around with you--sometimes for years.

And the good news is, you don't have to mean it. But, sweet friend, eventually, you probably will. My prayers for those I need to forgive may have started with, "Lord, help them go to heaven tonight," but today I find I can legitimately pray, "God, give them all the good things in their life that I want in mine." That progress did not come from giving in to rehearsing resentments day after day. It came from choosing, again and again, to forgive.

But the movie and I agree on that one truth, that in the end, forgiveness is *always* the least exhausting choice.

Lost and found

In four days my daughter and I, for her sixteenth birthday, are going to Paris. She has been looking forward to this for approximately 10 years. However, the original plan was to go with Daddy. But, now that she is going to be 16, we are realizing there are just certain parts of a Paris trip that might be better suited for a mom-daughter experience (perfume shops, cafes, shopping, and other girly adventures, for example). But I have to confess something to you--I am *scared*. Actually, today I am less terrified than I was a few months ago when we decided I would be the "adult" going.

I am a fairly confident person, so when I mention this to my friends, they assure me that I am fully capable of this task. This confounds me also. I finally figured out what it is that is giving me anxiety about this trip. I realized a few days ago that the answer is simple: I am afraid of *getting lost*. I am a real estate agent who uses google maps to get around my hometown where I have lived for over 20 years. So now, you are telling me, that I have to get my daughter and I safely around Paris using an actual paper map and getting directions from people who may or may not speak English? Sounds ominous.

Once I identified this fear, I was able to address the fact that ultimately, getting "lost" is not the end of the world. If it happens, I can simply take an Uber back to the hotel (a fancy hotel in Versailles that most anyone could find). End of story. No need to panic.

And now, since I have been pondering the idea of getting lost for several days, I have a few other thoughts on the matter. You know me well enough by now to know that I have to relate this to soul-level stuff. The first thing to remember is that you are not truly lost if you know where you are at the moment. You may not have intended to go there and it may not be where you want to stay, but being aware of your current location is crucial to being "un-lost." Being in the moment and embracing it can help you avoid feeling lost.

Maybe, just maybe, the place you are standing is not an accident.

Quite often, I have made detailed, extravagant plans to go one place and have ended up somewhere entirely different. God has a way of redirecting us when we plow ahead without Him. Maybe we are supposed to be in the very place we are trying desperately to get out of.

In spite of all that, there are times when I am legitimately "lost;" when I have landed in a place that no one should go alone and one should make every effort to avoid going again. I usually got there as a result of one of the following: 1) I was arrogant and refused to ask for directions. I didn't ask for wisdom from anyone, including God. I wanted to do it my way and only my way. 2) I didn't trust the Navigator. Even when I was instructed clearly by a Source that knows me better than I know myself, I doubted and ended up taking some wrong turns. 3) Sometimes I just got distracted. It wasn't an intentional, willful defiance. I just spaced out or was giving more attention to people and things around me than to where I was headed.

So as I anticipate going to Paris and as I consider moving forward in all areas of my life, I hear one clear message in my mind:

"Getting lost won't kill you. Staying lost just might."

I don't think anyone is immune from the possibility of "lostness." And maybe what you think of as "lost" is actually "found." God has a way of upsetting our apple cart. As long as we know where we are, we are exactly where we are supposed to be at that moment. We need to seek Him to find out if it's time to keep moving forward towards Him, turn around and retrace our steps back to Him, or simply enjoy the new scenery. No matter what we choose to do, we are not "lost." God promises direction. A way home. A way back to ourselves and to Him. He is that Way. In Him we can always be found.

Lost and found: Part 2

Well, it happened. My worst fear came true as soon as we reached Paris: we got lost. We had to take two different trains to reach our hotel which was about an hour and a half from the airport. After finally purchasing our train passes (post-13 hours of travel and remember, those people in France speak *French*) we jumped on the train that arrived at the spot where our train was scheduled to arrive. We hopped on and settled in, following the route mapped out on the wall of the train. We made several stops and were enjoying the scenery when my daughter alerted me that the stop we just passed was actually on a different line. Apparently, the route split and we realized were now headed in the wrong direction.

At the next stop we immediately disembarked and stood, perplexed, on a pretty much abandoned platform, wondering what to do next. There were only two people available to attempt to ask, in French, about how to get ourselves back on track. They were two college-age girls, so at least they seemed fairly harmless to two lost girls from Illinois. We mustered up our best French accents and asked, "Parlez vous Anglais?" ("Do you speak English?") And what do ya know!? They were from New Jersey! They spoke fluent English *and* French. They helped us figure out where we had gone wrong. It was an easy fix. We had to get on a train going backwards about two stops and transition to a different train in the same terminal. They had made the same mistake we had.

A couple minutes later, another train dropped off an older couple who had also gotten on the wrong train. Except they were from Spain and only spoke Spanish. They approached these same girls and even though it may sound like I am making this up, those two girls also happened to be fluent in Spanish. By the time we got to the new train, there was a nice little posse following these girls, asking them all kinds of questions and relying on them to get us where we needed to go.

The rest of the week was a series of seamless traveling from trains to Metros to Ubers. But as I was talking through real-life stuff with a friend yesterday, this situation came to me as a visual for how my life has often gone. Maybe yours too. There have been numerous times in my life when I have gotten on the wrong train. The wrong path. The path that leads to a destination that was not where I intended to land. Sometimes it was because I was hasty or not paying very much attention when I got on. I was living life without purposely seeking God's plan and giving too little thought or consideration to how my current decisions would affect the eventual outcome. Other times it was more intentional. I just thought I knew better than to get directions or advice from God or to seek wisdom from anyone else. Arrogance is often at the root of getting lost.

Whatever the reason, once we have gotten on the wrong path, the train that leads to destruction, we always have a choice. And God always provides a way out, a way off, a way back. And when we make that decision, He always provides the means to get ourselves on the right track. The first few times we may end up riding the train all the way to the end, with consequences and results that can be heartbreaking and devastating and cause us to grieve in our regrets. But hopefully, over time, we can do what my daughter and I did; we paid attention to the path we were on and immediately got off when we realized we were headed to the wrong part of town.

Let's be honest, we won't always make great decisions. That's just the reality of life. Our self-will and emotions and worldly desires often cloud our judgment. But hope is not lost. If we continue to work towards being spiritually fit by staying connected to a Power greater than ourselves, we can learn to identify when we are getting off-track and jump off the train. When we do this, we can pause, pray, and proceed to the proper route.

And I just *love* that just like God provided two English/French/Spanish-speaking college girls to come to the rescue of some lost and scared English/French/Spanish-speaking tourists, He will provide exactly what you need to get you to where you need to go. No lecturing. No shaming. No guilt trip. Just kind, gentle guidance. Following His lead and trusting His path as you begin your journey again.

"Life is"

"Life is Good"? Try "Life is Boring," "Life is Hard," Life is Dull." Now, wouldn't those make good slogans for a T-shirt line? Maybe it's because I am coming down from the thrill of being in Paris for a week, but I feel bored and tired and disinterested in my everyday life.

I realize I sound like a total brat but let me explain myself a bit and I think we can "reason things out" together…

"Greater love has no man than this, that a man lay down his life for his friend…I have called you friends." Jesus said that. But I don't think he was only referring to the day He physically gave up His life for us--His friends. Oswald Chambers points out that "it is far easier to die than to lay down the life day in and day out without the sense of high calling. We are not made for brilliant moments, but we have to walk in the light of them in ordinary ways."[32]

Even Jesus, the Son of God in the flesh, had very few brilliant moments. But for 30 years he laid out His life to do the will of His Father. He spent the majority of His time walking (a *lot* of walking), teaching, playing with children, studying, fishing, praying, and building furniture and cabinets and kitchen cupboards with His dad. We sometimes forget that He was a helpless baby, a toddler, and a brother and managed to survive the teenage years, all without sinning. Much of the preparation for his tiny, three-year stretch of ministry happened in the boring, dull, hard moments of life. And even those years weren't action-packed.

Maybe you are a little bit like me. I want to live with the energy that comes from living a heroic kind of life. I want the big without having to do the little. I want my spiritual life to be in order by today, my body to be in tip-top shape by tomorrow, and my book to be published by Thursday and for me to be on the speaking circuit by Friday. Instead, I have to "lay down my life." I have to do the small, hidden, seemingly insignificant tasks until those goals are reached. I have to rise and give God priority and permission to put into me what I need and root out what I don't need. And I have to do that consistently in order to grow up spiritually. I have to get up every stinkin' morning and work out, whether I feel like it or not. I have to write and revise and carve out moments to think and pray and prep while sitting alone on my couch. With no one watching or applauding or commenting.

I love the movie *Christmas Vacation*. At one point "Cousin Eddie" comes to Clark's house for a surprise visit (for an indefinite amount of time in his RV, with two wild kids and a slobbering dog). He has sold his house and bought an RV because he doesn't have a job. He hasn't had a job for several years because, according to his wife, "He's holding out for a management position."[33] There's little chance of a management position if you haven't proven that you can do the basics --like holding down a regular job, for starters. Don't be like Cousin Eddie. Stop believing that the only life that counts is the "good life."

Life is made up of lackluster moments. How we live in them is what matters. Life and all the moments of achievement and glory and accomplishment are the result of "laying down your life" on a daily basis. In the mundane and ordinary. Not dying for a great cause for everyone to see. It's important for us to remember this when we start to think that doing the dishes, mowing the lawn, cooking dinner, driving kids to soccer, taking out the trash, showing up for work day in and day out are boring and uneventful. If we, if *I*, think my life can only be enjoyable and fulfilling when the big stuff is happening, I will live with much disappointment.

"Life" is often sad and sometimes happy. It's occasionally fun and intermittently scary. It's painful and joyous and confusing and enlightening. It all counts. Maybe my T-shirt will simply say ***"Life Is."*** Today I will choose to "lay down my life." *All of it.*

Haunted house

Being a Realtor, I have had contact with dozens and dozens of home buyers. I never realized how many reasons there were not to buy a house. Some of the most common reasons are things like the yard being too small, the laundry room being in the basement or the wrong floor plan. Recently, I got a call from a buyer who was interested in a house I had listed. Bottom line--she wanted to know if anyone had died in the house. She was afraid it was haunted. She didn't end up buying it, even though her dogs visited the home so she could see if they had any reaction to a "presence" that might be lingering in the house. So, that was a first. And even though I am fairly certain that house wasn't haunted, I am beginning to believe that mine is. Well, specifically, my body-house. My soul.

According to Oswald Chambers, "We are all haunted by something, generally, by ourselves ..."[34] For a long, long time, I was haunted by resentments. Memories of people who I felt had betrayed me. People who had hurt my family in some way. Recollecting and rehashing painful experiences relentlessly invaded my mind day in and day out with no relief. I felt haunted. Unable to focus on the stuff in my life that *wasn't* so scary. I was moving around, doing the deal, but my mind was anxious and preoccupied with past events and offenses. After many intentional prayers for those people and for my angry heart to be softened and humbled, I was able to find some deliverance from that haunting.

But here's the deal: there is always something, or someone, waiting in line to take the place of that particular "presence." Our only solution is to be haunted by God. "The whole of our life inside and out is to be absolutely haunted by the presence of God."[35] The Bible puts it like this, "In Him we live, and move and have our being" (Acts 17:28). Since I read about this concept from Oswald Chambers (who wrote in the 1930s), I have been praying for God to haunt me. Because I have a very strong tendency to allow worry and fear to take up residence in me, penetrating every nook and cranny of my being. Chambers says, "If we are haunted by God, nothing else can get in, no cares, no tribulation, no anxieties. We see now why God so emphasized the sin of worry. How can we dare be so utterly unbelieving when God is round about us? To be haunted by God is to have an effective barricade against all the onslaughts of the enemy."[36]

When we are haunted by God, our enemies (whatever yours may be: fear, anxiety, worry, jealousy, anger, etc.) cower. If God's presence dwells and abides and consumes our being, there is no room left for such invasions. Invite Him to *haunt* you today.

I'm out of control!

This blog has been on my mind for about a year now. It addresses one of my worst character defects: *control.* Admitting the stronghold this defect has on me is just plain embarrassing. Nevertheless, I have the perfect illustration for *control* and it is high time I share it out loud.

Last summer we stayed at a resort in Florida. One afternoon my daughter and I rented one of those bicycles that has a bench seat, four wheels and two steering wheels. Do you have the picture in your head? Even though there were two steering wheels, only the one on the "driver's" side actually maneuvered the bike. Needless to say, I was stuck on the side with the "dummy" steering wheel, the one typically reserved for children who might otherwise steer you into a ditch. We had the bicycle for a half-hour. It just about killed me. I had zero control over where we went and any attempt to redirect our course was useless. If we got too close to a curb, I would madly turn the wheel with frustration. My daughter would point out, with the vast wisdom of a teenager who can't even drive a car yet, that my steering wheel was just for looks. It wasn't connected to anything. It was just there to make me feel like I had some semblance of control while in reality I was just wasting a lot of energy and sweating profusely (I mentioned we were in Florida in July, right?).

This is a great image of how I operate with God, regularly. He has full control of my life. He is in the driver's seat with a functioning steering wheel and I am wildly trying to make Him go where I want to go. I may feel like I am contributing but the reality is that my steering wheel isn't hooked up to anything. My job is to enjoy the ride and let Him take me where He wants to take me. I am fooling myself if I think that if I just put more effort and energy into it, I can somehow manipulate which direction I go.

I have a friend who has a couple of little children. One is about 10 and one is 7ish. Certainly neither is at an age to parent, and yet the older one occasionally thinks he knows what his mom should be doing to keep the younger one in line. Once when I was visiting, he came to his mom with some "information" on what his sister was doing as well as a few tips on how she might go about addressing the sister's behavior. My friend (who I am personally a little afraid of myself) gave him some good, calm advice right back, "Hey bud, how about if you let me parent your sister today? That OK with you? You can go ahead and take the day off." He sighed and ran off.

I feel a little bit like that 10-year-old. I think I have great ideas and also some pretty handy information that might help God do His job a bit more effectively. I mean, maybe there's something He hasn't taken into consideration in my particular situation (as if I am the first person to encounter such a dilemma). Me trying to tell God how it should be done better is like a 10-year-old telling his momma how to be a better parent. He believes that if only he were in control, things would run much smoother. That 10-year-old and I just keep right on trying to get our two cents in there.

I have been wondering since last year why I keep putting off writing this. I never really had a good answer except that when the time came, I would know. Well, let me tell you, this weekend, *I know.* God has provided some lovely and obvious opportunities for me to writhe in the sensation of having absolutely zero control of the people, places, and things around me.

And though I fought it for a couple days, I think I am ready to surrender. I am ready to just sit next to Him and let Him steer. I am not even going to pretend.

"Eat this, not that"

A few years ago a diet book came out called *Eat This, Not That*. Pretty self-explanatory. I think it would be hard to write an entire book outlining what should be common sense. Do we really need hard evidence that we should eat strawberries ("this"), not strawberry-flavored ice cream ("that") or a baked potato ("this"), not french fries ("that")? I realize there is more to the book than these kind of instructions, but humor me for a few minutes.

This morning I was reflecting on Step 7 of the 12 Steps of Recovery. It says, we "humbly asked God to remove our shortcomings."[37] We ask Him to take from us the character defects that cause us to "come up short" of His standard for us. And though I used to believe otherwise, today I don't see it so black and white. When we humbly ask Him to remove our shortcomings, we allow Him to choose which ones benefit us and which ones don't. My typical approach has been to give Him a list of things I don't like about myself and request that He take them away. Please take my selfishness, my stubbornness, my attempts to control and manage my image. But the more I learn about this step, a couple things occur to me …

The first is that when He does take something away, it needs to be replaced with something else. Theologian Richard Rohr says, "God's totally positive and lasting way to remove our shortcomings is to replace it with something much better, more luminous and more satisfying."[38] Otherwise we are left empty and are tempted to long for and crave those defects. Anything feels better than hollow. We have to be open and willing to receive His good and fulfilling gifts of "love, joy, peace, patience, kindness, goodness, gentleness, faithfulness and self-control."

The second thought that occurred to me is that it's not always an "all or nothing" scenario. Sometimes, when we are not spiritually fit or under the influence of addictive powers that are unhealthy for us, our assets actually become defects. They are too far down the dangerous end of the continuum. When God "removes our shortcomings," there may be times when He says to eat broccoli with lemon juice ("this"), not broccoli with cheese sauce ("that"). The good news is, we still get to eat broccoli (well, that's good news for some of you. I'm still wishing someone would tell me that if I eat nuts on my ice cream and not chocolate syrup that I can keep ice cream on my diet plan).

But you get my point, right? Sometimes He just needs to bring what appears to be a character defect back to its rightful place, turning it into an asset. For example, I have a friend who claims she has "helpful disease." She can't help but … *help* people. Helping people is not a defect of character when it is in its rightful place, but if she doesn't stay emotionally healthy and spiritually fit, her tendency is to *over*-help and turn this gift into something that doesn't benefit her or the "helpee." I have to be cautious not to take advantage of this, however, because I have been the recipient of a pair of great pants that she owned (after I told her they looked good on her) and an adorable purse she bought at a party (after I mentioned that my mom's identical purse had been set on fire by a candle).

The bottom line is this: Our job is to humbly ask. It's God's job to do the removing and replacing. That sounds easy, but for some of us, and especially those of us who like to feel in charge and in control and important, it is challenging. But what a relief if we can learn what our job is and what it is not. And be OK with what God takes and doesn't take. And what He tweaks instead of takes. "Eat This. Not That."

"Rephrase the question"

I have only been called in for jury duty once. And sometime soon I will tell you how I managed to get myself selected for a trial (because, apparently, playful attempts at clever banter with the judge are "frowned upon" in a court of law). But today I want to tell you a little bit about the case I was selected for. It was pretty awful. Not the crime itself, but the situation. A woman was suing a certain superstore that starts with a "W" and ends with "almart." It had been almost one year since the accident (she slipped and fell in a puddle of shampoo that had fallen off a shelf) and, here is the bad part, she was representing *herself*. Just let that sink in a moment. Even if she had the best lawyer money can buy, I am still fairly certain that losing was in her future. It was excruciating to watch this woman "play" lawyer.

By the end we, the jury, just felt sorry for her. The professional and powerful lawyer representing the superstore took full advantage of the fact that she had no idea how to argue her case. And the judge was no help. Every single time she made a statement or asked a question and the other lawyer objected, the judge would tell her to "rephrase the question/statement." That's when it got especially painful to watch. Bless her heart, she tried her best to think of three or four other ways to ask the exact same question, but she could never quite get her point across without being told to rephrase it, as if she had been to law school. In the end she was broken-down and humiliated.

Basically, she ended up losing, partly because she couldn't seem to express herself in a way that was acceptable to the judge or the cutthroat defense attorney.

Her *groanings*, her cries for help and for someone to truly "hear" her, fell on deaf ears. She had no chance before she even opened her mouth.

But unlike that woman, *we* do. Maybe not in the presence of a judge, but of *the* Judge. Before a God who is just, but also loving. And most importantly, a God who knows, before we even open our mouth, what we are trying to say. What we need. A God who doesn't expect us to know exactly what we want and to be able to express it flawlessly before He will even listen. Through God's clear Word to us, He tells us in Romans 8:23 that even when our own words are unclear, His spirit "intercedes for us with groans that words cannot express."

This is very good news. Because outside of a 650-word blog, I struggle with clarity. I am often hell-bent on getting what I want but at the same time am pretty certain that it doesn't line up with what I need. What I ask Him for may not be good for me. And that's on a good day! When I am under emotional duress, stand back! When my heart is in anguish and I can't see straight or focus on anything but the feelings weighing down on me, His Spirit in me steps in. He takes the jumbled letters of the alphabet in my head and puts them into the words He needs to hear. My "groanings" suffice. He knows and hears our pain, but "groaning" isn't reserved for just the bad stuff. By definition, "groaning" denotes a deep inarticulate sound conveying pain, despair, pleasure, etc. Have you ever been so overwhelmed by His goodness and blessings in your life that you were speechless? Again, His Spirit can communicate the depth and intensity of feelings we can't define with our meager vocabulary.

The best news in all of this is that when we can't trust ourselves to ask for what's best for us, we *can* trust that if we are humble before God, His Spirit will intercede on our behalf "in accordance with God's will." I truly want to live my life aligned with God's plan for me. I think most of us do at some level. It's ever so much richer than living life on self-will. Matthew 6:8 assures us that God knows what we need before we ask Him, before we ourselves know or are willing to admit what we need.

My "groaning" today comes from a deep place in my soul that wants God to know the fullness of my gratitude for being a Judge who understands what I am trying to say without making me repeatedly "re-phrase the question."

"That's gonna leave a mark"

I just can't stop thinking about mark. Or, more accurately, a mark. It started while listening to my iPod on my flight to Las Vegas. The band U2 was blasting the song "Magnificent" in my ears while Bono sang "Only love, only love can leave such a mark."[39] My schizophrenic mind then pulled up other files in my brain relating to the word "mark." Ever since Chris Farley uttered the words in the movie *Tommy Boy,* I haven't been able to bump or cut a body part without declaring, "Now *that's* gonna leave a mark!" (If you have never seen that scene, stop what you are reading and go directly to YouTube and check it out before continuing). After I went down that rabbit trail I remembered a client of mine who owns a tattoo parlor. His name is Mark and his email is "permanentmark." Get it? *Permanent Mark*? (I know, I am easily impressed). If I ever get a tattoo I am going to him based on that name alone. So, even though I want to take a nap on this flight, I just have to talk about *marks* for a few.

Unless we get a tattoo, or are married to Mark, most marks are not permanent. They may seem so at times, but usually there are ways to remove, remedy, or repurpose them. All of us have had defining moments, marking moments, in our lives. Events that threaten to stick with us forever. They damage in ways that feel pretty permanent. And left untreated, they indeed are. But, my friend, you have a Redeemer--One who wants to remove, remedy, or repurpose those marks. One who wants to leave you with a different kind of mark. I love how Bono says, "Only love can leave such a mark, only love can heal such a scar."[40] *God is that love.* Sometimes we falsely believe that *people* are that love, but the humanness of those people can cause that healing to be quite temporary. God's love is a permanent mark, leaving a scar as a reminder of where we once were when we were damaged. A mark that reminds us to trust in Him to be a salve for the wounds that we thought would ugly-us-up indefinitely.

Pure, unadulterated, healing love is a permanent gift from God. And yeah, "that's gonna leave a mark."

God doesn't chew gum

The other night a friend of mine, a college professor who teaches *real* writers how to write better, pointed something out to me. I told her I wish I had been able to write when some traumatic events from my past were happening. I indicated that maybe I could write about them now. She said, "*Now* you are thinking like a writer." I am not sure that she was referring to writing about trivial past events such as the one I am about to share with you, but nevertheless, here it goes …

I was about 10 years old and was beginning to take a "tap/jazz" class. I had never taken any class like this before and was very excited to choose a couple of leotards to wear to said class. One was pretty cute, robin egg blue with light pink tights. The other, and I have no idea what I was thinking or why my mother allowed this (though I suspect I wasn't an easy person to say "no" to back then, any more than I am now), but I choose a canary yellow leotard *and* canary yellow tights to go with it. Ten-year-old girls often go through a slightly pudgy, shapeless stage and I was right on target for that. So there's a lovely image. Tap shoes really topped off the outfit.

I entered the dance studio and quickly felt awkward, untalented, and very *very* bright. There were two other girls who seemed to be best friends nearby. I don't know what they really thought of me, but I sure felt like a third wheel trying to become part of that team. I tried my best to be friendly and make conversation. I truly can't even remember if they were nice to me, but I knew one thing: I desperately wanted to be their friend.

And here is where the memory sticks. After many failed attempts to get them to include me, to like me and acknowledge me, I finally came up with a solution that was iron-clad: I would buy them some gum. Yep. That should do the trick. When all else fails, just buy them some gum and that will break down all barriers and create life-long relationships. I am not sure if I ever actually did it. Probably not, because I had to get money from my mom and have her take me to the store and she, being *not* a lunatic, might have steered me away from such humiliation. My time in that class was short-lived. I never won those girls' affection and am sorely deficient at tap dancing to this day.

I still remember this because I occasionally feel myself trying to impress someone or win someone's approval even today. I used to work at a job where there were a couple of girls (OK...*women*) who I really wished would let me "in." Who would like and include me. I snicker because I said to myself, "Maybe I should buy them some gum." Because that's how I felt. Like a roly-poly 10-year-old in a neon yellow leotard. When I think this way, I know my identity is at risk. It means I am not finding my identity in what God, my Creator who loves me and includes me and accepts me for who I am right at this moment, thinks of me. I am depending on what other people think (or what I *think* they think) of me to feel secure.

Author and speaker Tony Campolo says, "Whatever the most important person in your life thinks of you is what you'll think of yourself."[41] If God is not that person, I am in big trouble. I love the slogan, "What you think of me is none of my business." It sounds rude at first but is actually a giant relief. It means we can relax and stop trying to impress people around us. That we can do the right thing without worrying about whether others will agree with us. We can be "OK" even when others around us don't think we are.

We can avoid an identity crisis because God's love and affection and stamp of approval never falter. And we can stop buying people gum (and don't quote me on this, but I am pretty sure God doesn't even chew gum).

God is like ...

Right now I am in real estate overload mode. I am working on several deals that need special attention, so the terminology and nuances of buying and selling houses are whirling around in my head consistently. But writing helps clear my head and focus on the parts of my job and life that truly matter. So, since I can't really block the real estate thoughts, I figured I might as well make good use of them. Sit for a few and join me in my maelstrom of thoughts on how God is like various players in the Real Estate Game.

God is like a Home Inspector. But let me set it up for you. If you haven't sold or tried to sell a house lately, here's how it goes. You are given a list of 23 areas that you can mark as either Yes, No or Not Applicable. Your agent cannot help you with that at all. Only you can give an honest answer to the questions that are on this list. In the past few years, a new question has been added and you will be relieved to know that a seller is required to disclose whether or not there was ever a methamphetamine lab in the house. Phew! As a seller, you reveal any defects that you are aware of and then give an explanation for them. Then, after your house is under contract, the buyer will send in a home inspector who will spend several hours searching for everything that is wrong with your house that you didn't even know about. It's a nerve-wracking thing for a seller and they are often surprised that there has been mold lurking in their basement and that their toilets flush backwards.

In this way, as I said, God is like a home inspector. There are many defects we have that we are fully aware of. But then, He takes it to the next level. He searches the nooks and crannies of our hearts and souls and finds dry rot and hot electrical wires and gas leaks and termites and all kinds of things that threaten our "house." Dangers we didn't even know about. Defects like pride, image-management, dishonesty, greed, lust, and jealousy. Defects that aren't as obvious to the casual observer but can cause structural damage to our lives if left unaddressed.

God is also like a buyer. A really *easy* buyer. One who sees the results of the home inspection report and the laundry list of flaws and imperfections and *buys it anyway.* He buys it AS-IS. I just love those kinds of buyers. They understand that every house has its issues and don't expect a 100-year-old house to present itself like new construction. He has bought us at a great price. Actually, I am fairly sure we would "under-appraise" for what He sacrificed to make us His own.

And, He is like a seller. He has a list of disclosures in His Word. He reveals everything about His House, which is to say, Himself. He shares it thoroughly, honestly, and freely. It is our job, our privilege, to do the inspecting. There are many characteristics of God that are obvious.

Anyone can tap into them if they give it just the tiniest bit of effort. His love and compassion and forgiveness are available to anyone who asks. But it's when we take extra time to explore His House that we really find the beauty of what's often hidden from plain sight. Luckily, we are always pleasantly surprised by our findings.

When we pray and meditate and read and open up our being to His will and wisdom, we experience His presence intimately. We begin to anticipate what we will find around the next corner of our relationship with Him.

Today I am grateful for what God can teach me about Himself, even in the midst of circumstances that seemingly have nothing to do with spiritual things. I am reminded that this is how I stay in constant contact with a God who is not just interested in my *spiritual* life, He is interested in my *life*. All of it. And today He and I are gonna do some serious real-estating together.

What is it that *you* and God will be doing?

Goodwill ranting

Let's talk about our feelings. Or at least my feelings. I really am not good at identifying feelings. I have been through hours of therapy over the years and one of the biggest takeaways has been that I am terrible at addressing, accepting, identifying, acknowledging, and sharing my feelings. I am really good at expressing my thoughts and opinions, but *apparently*, those aren't the same thing. I am not lying when I tell you that I actually have a list I printed off a website (something like *Feelings for Dummies*) so I could peruse a list of feelings and check them off if I was experiencing them. Like multiple choice. So, now that I have laid the foundation for my entry today, let us continue …

Warning: this blog may be a bit "all over the place," but that seems appropriate since we are talking about feelings. Let me start by telling you about some of my history of *not feeling* or at least feeling emotions that are mislabeled.

I remember having a conversation with my husband Blake years ago about how angry I was at some friends. I was fired up and indignant about being left out of information I felt everyone else knew but me. I was ready to just move on and do life without any friends at all. Who needs 'em!? Blake listened patiently for a bit and then said something like, "Is it possible that your feelings are just hurt and that makes you sad?" And just like that, I burst into tears. He was right, I was sad and wounded. Anger just felt like a powerful way to express myself. Those other kinds of emotions feel vulnerable and that is extremely hard for me.

Next: When I had leukemia and didn't know it yet, there were several symptoms that were unexplainable.

No one, including me, could put a finger on anything that might lead to a diagnosis or solution. I was tormented with possible scenarios. I was aware of myself enough to know that life had thrown our family some pretty big curveballs over the past couple of years and that I was barely coping with them.

One symptom of my stress was that I didn't feel anything at all. No highs. No lows. No joy, anger, relief, sadness, fear. It was all the same: numbness. I began to believe that maybe the permanent lump in my throat was a cluster of emotions that were "stuck" in me. That my many other symptoms were my body's way of cluing me in that I had some junk that needed to be brought to the surface. I'd stuffed it down so long, it was logical to me that it would start manifesting itself physically. Unfortunately, it was actually leukemia, but the other conclusion still makes sense to me.

Though I am getting better at identifying my emotions, mostly due to 12 Step recovery principles, I still struggle identifying, dealing with, and accepting my emotions. I was reminded of this in full color when I was in California helping my college student get settled. More specifically, I was kicked in the teeth with the realization that I had been stuffing some significant feelings about him being 21, not needing me, living in an apartment, and probably (and hopefully) never living at home again. And here's the main problem with not dealing with your emotions as they come--they tend to sneak up and surprise you when you are not expecting them.

Something cracks the dam and they come gushing out sideways in the middle of Goodwill over a $9.00 lamp and a $3.00 picture frame. You act like a lunatic because you chose to "deal with it later" when you felt that sadness and fear and concern come on you during the summer. But today is the "later" and you have dozens of emotions that are spinning in you like a tornado. And the damage is the same, *random and powerful.*

While I was in California, when circumstances were threatening to overwhelm me, a wise friend said, "Sometimes you just have to do your job. You can set your emotions on the shelf for a bit. They can come out later for a visit. But they can't visit right now." That was a very helpful perspective that got me through the next few hours of crucial decisions I had to make. But as I thought more about it, I said to her, "The problem for me is that I tend to forget to invite them to come for a visit so they just pop in and surprise me when I least expect it!" Like, in the middle of Goodwill, for Pete's sake.

As I sat to write this morning I prayed and asked God what exactly He wanted me to say. I was floundering a bit between a few struggles I have been having that I wanted to get out of my head. And, as usual, He showed me. I was leaning towards writing about this "feelings" crap, but wasn't convinced that's what He had in mind. I turned to the reading for this date in my Recovery book and I started to cry. Here is what one of the paragraphs said:

"... I have learned that feelings aren't shortcomings. The true nature of my problem was my stubborn refusal to acknowledge feelings, to accept them, and to let them go. I have very little power over what feelings arise, but what I choose to do about them is my responsibility. Today I can accept my feelings, share about them with others, recognize that they are feelings, not facts, and then let them go."[42]

God gave me feelings and the ability, with His help, to handle each of them. Sequestering them on a shelf or shoving them deep down in my soul only leaves me susceptible to surprise visits. It's ever so much easier to deal with my feelings one at a time. Maybe you struggle with this too. Let me know if you need my list of emotions for dummies and join me in doing the work of identifying, accepting, and letting go of your feelings before they do what mine did last week. Trust me, it's not pretty.

"Hypocrisy." I hate that word!

"How you do your life is your real and final truth, not what ideas you believe."[43]

-Richard Rohr

This sentence has been invading my thoughts since I read it a couple of weeks ago. I can't shake it, and for good reason. It challenges everything I think and act on every minute of the day and sometimes in the middle of the night. What it clarifies for me is the blunt reality that what I say I believe is often very different from how I act. And I am not just referring to the times I say I believe in taking good care of my body and then proceed to eat approximately half a bag of chips and salsa. Or how I say I believe it's imperative to start my day on spiritual footing but hit the snooze so many times that I bolt awake in a frenzied rush just to make it to my first appointment, without even a flippant prayer or passing thought of *God's* plan for my day. These may seem like silly examples. There are many bigger ways that I have not lived out what I believe.

But here's a question that has been pestering me, or rather, pursuing me, lately: what about the tiny dark places that only God and I know about? My life might look good on the outside, to my readers and friends and, most of the time, my family. But if I am honest, there are moments when I am not living what I say I believe. I am living out what I *really* believe and those two are often quite opposite. There is a strong word for this that is stinging and harsh, but nevertheless, accurate. Hypocrisy. I think it's fair to say that we hate hypocrisy. Many people have stumbled in their quest for God because of people who say they are God-followers but live in a way that is unkind, unloving, judgmental, arrogant. I don't want anything to do with that category of "Christian."

Hypocrisy means "the practice of claiming to have moral standards or beliefs to which one's own behavior does not conform"(Merriam-Webster Dictionary). Well, that pretty much sums up what Richard Rohr was saying: "How you *do your life* is your real and final truth, not what ideas you believe." Paul says as much to the people in the Church of Rome, a couple thousand years ago. He says, "You who teach others, do you not teach yourself? You who preach against stealing, do you steal? You who say that people should not commit adultery, do you commit adultery?" You get the gist. Most of us feel pretty safe to answer those questions with self-righteous confidence.

However, lately I have been asking myself questions like, "You who teach others not to worry, do you worry? You who say resentments will kill you, do you hold grudges? You who say you believe God will provide all your needs, do you feel jealous of what your friends have? You who say you trust God to direct your life, do you live in fear of the future? You who say God loves your kids more than you do, do you fret over their safety and life choices? You who say that living in God's will is the best option for peace and serenity, do you work fervently to manipulate and control the people around you so that *your* will is done instead?"

The answers are embarrassing. According to Webster's Dictionary, I am a hypocrite. That word makes me feel sick. And humbled. And repentant. I do not want to be a hypocrite.

In order to do that, I must live "as if" I actually believe what I say I believe. It's one thing to have occasional temptations to worry. That's normal. But if I live in worry, that is opposite of what I say I believe to be true about God and His ability and willingness to help me not worry. It's normal to be tempted by all the questions I posed above, but to live in them and coddle them and make it a habit or lifestyle, is hypocrisy.

I have to pray, maybe a thousand times a day, prayers like:

"God, I feel afraid, I am turning that fear over to You."

"God, I feel worried about money, I am turning that worry over to You."

"God, I feel unhappy in my circumstances, I am turning my discontent over to You."

"God, I feel scared for my kids' futures, I am turning them over to You."

Now you try:

"God, I feel ______________, I am turning ____________________ over to You." AMEN

Myself! Myself! Myself!

I was talking with a friend a couple of days ago who has a story that rivals any memoir I have ever read about dysfunctional families. I told her she should write her own book. She basically told me, "No way! I don't want to sit down and think about any of that on purpose!" I get it. I know the feeling. There are some things that we would rather not reflect on intentionally. I bring this up, because although it's minor compared with much of what I avoid thinking about, I have been avoiding writing about my follow-up story from last week's blog entry on hypocrisy. I am not 100% sure why, but I have been finding a lot of other, more pressing things to fill my time. I have an inkling that it is because it was exhausting and profound and difficult.

So, let's get on with it. (Read the previous entry if you haven't already, otherwise I might sound crazier than usual). Last weekend I wasn't planning to write. It was early morning and I was heading out of town to do some Homecoming dress shopping with my daughter and mom. I had a couple hours to get ready. I was doing my typical reading routine when the topic fell in my lap. Hypocrisy. Do I really live like I believe what I say I believe? I say God can take away my fears and worries but do I let those feelings consume me? Refer to that blog for more lovely examples of my duplicity. I mentioned, as a solution, that I can pray,

"God, I am feeling worried about __________, I am turning my __________ over to You." That's practical. I can try that. That would help me at the very least turn my attention to Someone more powerful than I am who can actually help. I made a promise to put this into practice in the future.

The curious thing about the future is that it starts immediately. And so it did. Almost as soon as I posted my entry, I checked my emails. I saw one that scared me to death. My mind went in to full "figure it out" mode and my brain started spinning information around and around. It was fear mixed with worry mixed with a terrible sense of being powerless and having no control. And the (potential) consequences were huge. Of course, my head went to the worst-case scenario and I literally felt sick and distracted and panicked. I have never had such an intense physical reaction to "information."

But then … I remembered what I say I believe. And what I had just written. I had no choice. I had to practice what I preached if I could look any of you in the face ever again. I knew I had an entire day to spend with two of my favorite people doing something fun and significant. I didn't want to let my fear and worry of what might happen in the future hijack my serenity for the whole day. I have most definitely done that before, with deep regret. So I reviewed the first three steps of Recovery in my head. I have heard them summed up like this:

Step One: I CAN'T

Step Two: GOD CAN

Step Three: I THINK I'LL LET HIM

This became my mantra for the day. I said it out loud and in my head at least 1,000 times. It would be lovely if once would cut it, but my tendency is to turn it over and take it back, turn it over and take it back. I find it amusing, and telling, that about half of those 1,000 recitations came out backwards the first time around. I would attempt to say it and I would say, "I *can*. Wait, no, I mean, I *can't*." I just so badly want to think I *can*. I can fix it. I can control it. I can change it. I can solve it.

When my oldest son was about two we took a swim class together. It was torture, for both of us. He couldn't swim at all but he developed his own little mantra that echoed in the kiddie pool area for the entire lesson: "My-self! My-self! My-self!" He wanted me to let him down even though he couldn't swim or touch. I knew this but he was not believing any of it. He was convinced he would be safe. I was just holding him back from success in his two-year-old mind.

This is my typical reaction to God when things get stressful. "My-self! My-self! My-self!" It's a dangerous and naive reaction. But I have to tell you that last Saturday, when stress and anxiety threatened my serenity and ability to be fully present with people I love, I tried doing the opposite. And it worked. I still felt fear sneaking up on me throughout the day, beckoning me to jump in with both feet, but I chose differently. I chose to trust Him. I repeated, "I can't. God can. I think I'll let Him," until I climbed into bed that night and throughout the weekend. The situation was not and is not "fixed," but my fears are diminished, and I am not frozen with dread (does this happen to anyone else?).

I am determined to continue this practice of living as an Anti-Hypocrite. It's much more palatable and will look much better on a T-shirt.

Timing is everything

"The waiting is the hardest part."[44]

-Tom Petty (1950-2017)

It feels like it's been a long time since I wrote last. Which is interesting to me since I have been reflecting on the concept of "time and timing" over the past few days. These thoughts on timing came to me in a very profound and illuminating way as I sat on my couch … admiring my fingernails. They are rockin' right now! They are long and strong and borderline dangerous to myself and others. But, this hasn't been the case for the past two years. I think it was the chemo that caused my nails to be flimsy and splitting. They hardly grew at all, but if they did, they would soon peel or break. The perplexing thing is, I haven't even been doing anything to remedy that problem. And all of a sudden, they are back to normal. It's like my body finally got rid of whatever was in me that was causing them to shatter. Nothing profound, it was simply "time."

Since then, everything I read seems to point me to time and timing. The longer I live, the more aware I am that so much of life is all about timing. Which is unfortunate, because I want what I want and I usually want it right now. I want to work out and be in shape by tomorrow or at least by the weekend. I want to read a self-help book and be organized, efficient, and successful by the time I finish chapter one. And those are the simple wants. I also want to pray for the people I am worried or stressed about and see results in a reasonable amount of time (I like to be fair and give God a few weeks). I try my best to understand why some people seem to get "better" quicker than others. Whether it's from cancer or mental illness or addiction or any kind of stronghold. The big question for me seems to be, "How long, Oh Lord?"

There is a saying in Recovery programs that has a good answer for those who lament not arriving in the program sooner. Someone new thinks of all the years they suffered alone, without any tools or people who understood their pain. An old-timer will tell them, "You got here right on time." Because timing is everything. If you show up before your soul is ready and willing to hear and receive help, it will fall on deaf ears. I think it's this way in all of life, really. The Bible uses a couple of phrases that indicate that there is a time for everything (not only from the popular song from Ecclesiastes and the Byrds telling us "there is a time be born, a time to die, a time to kill and a time to heal …"[45]). One is "the fullness of time" and the other is "for such a time as this." Both imply that there are certain events and attitudes that have to be established before something can happen. Until all the pieces are in place, the results won't come.

We have such limited knowledge and access to what those pieces look like. They are an accumulation of interactions, relationships, behaviors and choices of thousands of people. We are interwoven with one another in ways we will never know, yet will still be affected by. The ripples run far and wide.

This is helpful for me to remember because, as I said, I like to see some progress. I hate waiting. I read something the other day (because, of course, God gave me about four different readings that all addressed "time." He is funny like that!) in which the author said something like this: How often I still find myself impatient with the pace of life. But today, when things don't happen according to my schedule, I can accept that there may be a reason...I can keep in mind that waiting time doesn't have to mean wasted time. Even times of stillness have lessons to teach me...I can accept the pace of change today, knowing it will bring both times of active involvement and periods of quiet waiting.

My need to be in control severely hinders me from being a better "waiter." I want to control how other people change, how my circumstances change, how I change and most importantly at what rate it all happens. My need for immediate gratification doesn't help either. "Now" is one of my favorite words.

An excerpt from *Streams in the Desert* says it this way: "Waiting on Him exercises your gift of grace and tests your faith. Therefore, continue to wait in hope, for though the promise may linger, it will never come too late."[46] When I try to rush results or manipulate circumstances to go my way or on my agenda, I show complete lack of trust in God's plan and demonstrate an exaggerated view of my own. Today I will let God set the pace.

But I trust in you, O Lord; I say "you are my God, my times are in your hands."

PSALM 31:14, 15

Four winning ways to worry

It feels so good to be back! Did you miss me? Remember when God and I and you all kicked leukemia in the butt? Well, while I was unconscious and intubated in ICU, apparently my mom promised me that if I didn't die, she would take my sister and me to Hawaii when I got better. Last week was that "better" and we spent nine amazing days celebrating not dying! I thought of you often while I was in Hawaii. We'll get back to that in a moment.

Awhile back, I signed up to receive a "word of the day" email since, as I write, I feel a yearning for better, smarter ways to express myself. Today my word was *nuncupative*. Never heard of it? Me either. It means, "spoken rather than written: oral" (Merriam-Webster Dictionary). I thought, that's what my blogs were like while I was in Hawaii--nuncuputive! I was with my mom and sister and we had several conversations that would qualify as a blog entry.

So, for better or for worse, here is the first entry, post-Hawaii. I know you will be shocked to hear me write again on the topic of worry. But as it turns out, being five hours earlier than where I live and an ocean away provides several new and improved modes of worry. I have experience with a couple of them, but it turns out they are heightened when you are 4,214 miles from home "as the crow flies" (that's what Siri tells me).

The two basics types of worry are 1) not getting what you want and 2) losing what you have. In regard to not getting what I want, I realized I developed a way to worry that isn't just about fear of what *might* happen, but more specifically, about what *might not* happen. And by what might not happen I mean it involves my expectations. I expect my kids to graduate and get good jobs and not live at home forever and ever-Amen. I expect my job to be successful and to move up and to the right. I expect my friends to call once in a while and invite me out. I expect my body to look like a 21-year-old, OK, how about 30-year-old, even though I am 47. I expect to be more mature and kind and generous and honest as I age and grow and learn. And I worry. I worry that those things might not actually happen, and God forbid, that they might happen but not in the way I have mapped out in my little head.

And let's just graze for a moment on the fear and worry that comes from losing what I already have. Even though my life isn't perfect, it's pretty good today. What if, in the blink of an eye, it all changes. I have lost many things in the past few years that really side-swiped me. My health being up at the top of that list. As much as I fear not getting what I want in the future, it can also be terrifying to think of everything changing. Today, while it isn't perfect, is also not terrible. And I know how to deal with today because I am in it. What if any of it should go away?

So, those two are pretty common types of worry and ones I hear others talk about regularly. Lucky for you I have identified a couple more, less commonly addressed types of worry to add to your list.

You can worry about what *might have* happened in the past. While we were in Hawaii we went on a dinner cruise, which in reality was a roller coaster ride of five-foot waves the majority of the time, up the Na Pali Coast. We had a wonderful and safe time. The next day my sister pointed out how crazy it is that boats can float. The physics of it all started freaking her out. And those waves? Oh my gosh, we could have died! How could a young captain and a marine biologist from the crew save 40 people? The thought of what could have happened started freaking us *all* out! And to top it off, my sister had to leave a day early. After she had been in the air for three hours, the captain announced that they would be back to their original location within the hour. The plane was having mechanical trouble. They sweated bullets for the next hour and after they landed safely, they were towed to the gate while fire trucks and ambulances stood by on the runway, "just in case." Now, that there will give one pause to think about what *might have* happened.

And I just love this last one. I actually think I found a loophole. God says to only worry about today. Meaning, what's happening at this very moment. Well, about 8:00 in the morning, Hawaii time, I found myself worrying about a test one of my kids had later that day. When it hit me; it *is* later today in Illinois! I was free to worry to my heart's content. It seemed like worrying about the future when it is actually the present has to be OK, right?

But, like I said about this blog, for better or for worse, God has the same answer for you regarding worry--don't do it. He says don't worry 365 times in the Bible. Do the math. He says to be anxious for nothing, but in everything give praise.

The only way to keep our minds and hearts from being overwrought with worry of any variety is to be grateful and trust Him. Be grateful for what we have and will have, even if it doesn't fulfill our expectations. Be grateful for what we had and how long we had it, even if we lose it. And be grateful for and trust His sovereign (supreme, absolute, unlimited, boundless, ultimate, unconditional) will for our individual lives.

So, there you go. I have outlined a few ways you didn't even know you could worry. I am sure you have a few of your own up your sleeve. Regardless of how many avenues you find to worry, remember: the solution is always the same.

My drug of choice

Just based on principle, I probably shouldn't be writing right now. But I feel like the only way to clear my head is to reason things out on paper so I don't go insane. Saturdays are hard for me because there is no routine. No agenda. And my family seems to be fine with that. But I am not. I have a hard time relaxing and put expectations on myself, which often spill over and soak my family, to be productive.

Productivity is my drug of choice. I can be held captive by it and render myself immobilized if I don't engage in it. Once I get a hit from it, I can feel the tension leave and the relief come. I am acutely aware of it on this cold, windy Saturday morning. I have no obligations and have ample time to read and write and relax with my coffee.

And yet, on the way to my spot on the sofa, I felt the overwhelming pull to "get a few things done." I did all the dishes while the coffee brewed (because God forbid I waste time simply waiting). Then I scurried from countertop to countertop, picking up stray objects and trying to figure out where they belong. After I got my coffee, I headed to the living room and decided I could quickly sort through the videos, DVDs, and books stored in the TV stand. About an hour after I set out to read and pray I was finally situated. I sat there, books in lap, coffee in hand, feeling like I had earned the right to finally just "be."

I don't know when this mindset took over my thinking. I remember talking to one of my teachers when I was in high school about his summer plans. He said that he made it a point to do one productive thing each day of his summer break. At the time, that seemed very noble and wise. So apparently my productivity addiction had not kicked in yet.

Thirty years later, I think, "ONE thing?!?! Really? If I am not feeling productive most of my day, I feel like I am failing." Even when I am relaxing, I don't feel very relaxed. I was watching TV in bed last night. TV. Bed. Both relaxing by nature. But at one point I realized I was tense and my shoulders were raised up and tight. I just seem to have trouble letting myself do something "unproductive" and enjoy it. I am not bragging either. That's not a good character trait to have. No one likes to be uptight. No one likes to be around people who are uptight.

I think a lot of this dependence I have on being productive stems from a false belief that I adopted somewhere along the way in my faith journey. I am still unlearning the notion that somehow my good behavior, my accomplishments, and my responsible choices are what God is looking for from me. While those things can't be thrown out the window entirely, they are not the basis for being in right standing with God. He alone does that for me. I have spent many years learning how to think differently. Obviously, the transformation process is slow. One step forward, two steps back.

Today, I am determined to try to relax and be present when I have the opportunity to do so, rather than to feel like I should be doing something different like cleaning or sorting or working. I am getting ready to run errands with my teenage daughter (and what, I ask, could be more relaxing than that!? ☺). I have a lot to do around the house (tasks I have made up to feel productive) but instead, I am going to ride with her and practice being present. Practice being grateful that she invited me. Practice being "unproductive" and being OK with it. I think it's exactly what God wants from me.

God is repetitive

A couple weeks ago I was in Hawaii. Sigh …

As we drove to the beach on our last day there, my mom and I had a discussion about Hawaiian words. How I can't pronounce any of them properly, for starters. I mean, how would you pronounce Kapaa or Poipu or Lihue? (However you said it, I can pretty much guarantee that's not it.) I might as well have been trying to speak French. Also, as we went through the spelling of the various cities and areas we visited, we noticed a few things. There are some letters they rarely if ever use (s, t, and r for example) and some that they use repeatedly (k, w, p, m and *lots and lots* of vowels).

Fast forward about an hour as we were lying in the sun. We started talking about a study my mom was doing. It happened to be written by one of my favorite authors, Beth Moore. This led us to bring up Anne Lamott, another favorite author of mine. I told my mom that a couple people have told me that my writing reminds them of hers. My interpretation of that compliment is that it's mostly because we are both pretty honest about our own messed up selves and tend to land on similar topics like grace and love and vulnerability.

But there is a huge difference in that she is a real writer who uses smart words and creative and intentional descriptive sentences that are simply way out of my league. My blogs are like the Walmart version of her Ralph Lauren writing. And that's when it hit me and made me laugh out loud; I am like the Hawaiian version of Anne Lamott! There are just some words and letters she uses that I will never, ever be able to use. And most of all, I am Hawaiian in that I repeat the same few words over and over and over. I use words like "like" and "thing" and "very" and "soooo much." My descriptive repertoire (I had to look up how to spell that!) is sorely lacking and simplistic.

My vocabulary is not the only thing that is repetitive. The more I write, the more I see the pattern. My topics are also repetitious. Any given blog you read will address the issues of worry, anxiety, trust, fear, control, grace, and acceptance. And to be honest, while that used to cause me to feel dumb and narrow, I now feel like I am in good company. Because you know who else is repetitive? God. And if this is one way I can be more like Him, I'll take it.

If you have ever read the Bible, or even if you haven't, you should know that even though there are approximately 807,361 words in the Bible, they tend to highlight certain themes over and over and over in different ways. The main two topics that run throughout the Bible are 1) love God and 2) love people. God also regularly addresses how we should handle worry, anxiety, fear, control, and how to live a life of peace and contentment as we trust His will over our own. It's rather repetitious when you get right down to it.

I repeat myself because I struggle with the same tendencies on a regular basis. The tendency to let worry and fear dominate, resulting in complete lack of trust in God's plan for me and the world around me. The tendency to control, to force solutions so that life works out the way I want it to or make people around me live up to my expectations. The tendency to withhold unconditional love and grace and judge others as if I were the great "I AM." From what I have heard from readers, I am not alone in these tendencies.

But God has gone ahead of us and given us His words of comfort and wisdom to help us navigate this repetitious life-cycle we are riding. He gives us the tools and promises to find relief from these areas, if we choose to use them. He knows it's a life-long battle for us, which is why He repeats Himself. He tells us the answers in a thousand different ways so He can get His main messages across in just the way we need to hear it.

I have a strong tendency to forget to keep the main things the main things. *Thank God* He is repetitive.

Inside out

I've heard it said that our outer world is often a reflection of our inner world. Which is to say that the symptoms of outer chaos and clutter and lack of focus can alert us to what is happening in our souls. I believe that and have found it to be true on more days than I care to admit. However, there is a big "but" attached to the solution to that …

And I almost fell for it last week. Outer chaos may very well be an indication that there is something askew on the inside, but the "but" of that is that no amount of order, organization, updating, or putting your house/office/bank account/room/desk/car/yard in order can substitute for addressing what's festering in your soul. The unrest can only be settled from the inside out.

In the past couple of weeks I have been in the process of moving my college-age son out of his room in the basement and moving my 17-year-old into it. This requires total upheaval and storing and sorting of two entire rooms and years of accumulated memorabilia. Once I completed that task we also rearranged and distributed furniture and electronics from the toy room and then painted and re-accumulated re-fabbed furniture (by me) to put in the newly painted (also by me) guest room that used to belong to my 17-year-old. Near the end of the madness, I actually caught myself feeling hopeful because it was almost over, and thinking, "Hang in there, Heather. Once you get this all organized and completed everything is going to be OK." The busy-ness and exhaustion and feelings of subtle anxiousness will melt away. Well, I am 99.9% done with this overhaul and guess what? I am not 99.9% better.

Here's what I learned: If I don't want to face certain situations or feelings, staying busy with projects and people and entertainment are excellent distractions. If I am afraid of looking at how I might need to change or adapt or what I might need to let go of, a good makeover (on my body or my home) works wonders. But eventually, when it's all said and done, I am left with me, myself and I to deal with.

I was thinking about this while running errands today. This problem manifests itself a couple of different ways in me. There are times when I over-schedule and allow very little margin so that I don't have time to think about areas of my life that are upsetting to me. It's called avoidance. I go to coffee and the store and work later than I should and watch movies until I can't keep my eyes open.

I know there is something causing me to feel unsettled but don't have the heart to handle it in a healthy way just yet. Then there are other times when I go a couple weeks in a frenzy of meetings and events and appointments before it occurs to me that maybe my unrest and lack of serenity might be coming from somewhere deep in my soul that is trying to flag me down. It's flailing and floundering and needs attention--stat!

Even now, as I write and reflect, I can feel the pull of productivity and validation through maintaining a full schedule--through getting stuff done. Sitting here on this couch, sharing, and looking inward is simply unacceptable (this is what my brain is telling me). But my spirit, God's Spirit whispering to me, tells me otherwise. It tells me *how* I go through life is more important than the *what*. And I can't do the *what* well if the *how* of my soul is running around like the Tasmanian Devil. I'm just sayin'.

"Though the doors were locked ..."

By now, some of you have read enough of my blogs to understand my unique daily reading plan. I could market said plan as "Rabbit Trail Reading Plan" or "ADD Reading Plan," both catering to busy, scattered, impatient, and focus-challenged individuals who are doing the best they can to grow up mentally, spiritually, and emotionally.

At any rate, here's how it looks for me. I read approximately four different books each morning. Each one has a daily entry that is shorter than most of the blog posts I write. While I am reading, I underline like crazy. I look up words I don't understand or that intrigue me. And I look up any references to Bible verses that are highlighted. When I look up those verses, I truly love it if I have already underlined them in my Bible (as if I were going to receive a prize or something). I also read what comes before and after those verses and occasionally end up reading a few chapters or other verses I have underlined around it. All that to segue into telling you about what I read the other day. And I couldn't stop crying.

Just a brief description of what's going on in John 20:26--You have probably heard the descriptor of someone who is skeptical or leery about something as being a "doubting Thomas." This passage is where that phrase comes from. After Jesus was killed and came back from the dead, He appeared to a few of His disciples. Poor Thomas. He wasn't there. So they told him about it and a paraphrase of what he said went something like, "What-ever, dudes. I'll tell you what; I have heard these rumors already and seen the posts on Instagram. You know they can make anything look real with photoshop, right? But until I see him with my own eyes and touch the holes where they nailed him to that cross, I'm not buying it." A week goes by and the disciples, including Thomas this time, are chillin' in someone's living room.

"And though the doors were locked,
Jesus came and stood among them."

"And though the doors were locked ..." That's the part that made me stop. Made me sob, actually. Because that is the God I believe in. Too often we picture Jesus as standing at the door of our hearts and knocking patiently. Wondering if we are home, hating to bother us with His measly gift of, um, forgiveness of sin and eternal life. This image probably comes from a frequently abused verse--"Behold, I stand at the door and knock "--that is often used to entice someone to turn their life over to the care of God. Spoiler alert: that verse was written to a church full of Christians that needed to get its act together. It wasn't about the heart of an individual who hadn't met up with the wonder of God yet.

The God I believe in and am abandoned to is not like a door-to-door salesman or a person who walks and knocks on neighborhood doors getting signatures to support his political agenda. He isn't politely tapping while I hide behind the curtain, peaking out the window, hoping he gives up soon and moves on. He's a God who pursues.

He knows we are home and He isn't leaving until we open the door. He knows what He offers is not only free (to us, not at all to Him) but the best gift we could ever receive. His grace and love and mercy are indeed priceless. Too often we are resistant to letting Him in. Sometimes it's because we are afraid. Sometimes it's because we are selfish and want to live by our own will. Sometimes, I think much of the time, it's because we think we are not worthy of the gift. That we have screwed up too often and in ways that seem irreparable.

The God I believe in, not to frighten you, is one who will find a way in *even though the doors are locked.* He will go through a window or jimmy the dead-bolt or come down the chimney. He is what the English poet Francis Thompson called "The Hound of Heaven."

As John Francis Xavier O'Conor wrote, "As the hound follows the hare, never ceasing in its running, ever drawing nearer in the chase, with unhurrying and unperturbed pace, so God follows the fleeing soul by His Divine grace." And even though, for a plethora of reasons, we try to hide and run and lose this Hound, He "unwearyingly follows ever after, till the soul feels its pressure forcing it to turn to Him alone in that never ending pursuit."[47]

You see, like a lover who knows without a doubt that you are destined to be together, God will passionately and fervently pursue you. You can run and hide and curse and reject, but those are hurdles He can handle. He is not hunting you down to punish or shame you. He is coming to bring the love, acceptance, peace, and joy you have been looking for in other things or other people.

Dear friend, I hope you can feel my two hands on your cheeks as I hold your face close to mine and tell you with a tender and emphatic whisper: "*Though your doors are locked,* He will find a way in. And that's not a threat, it's a beautiful promise."

Surefire weight-loss plan

Let's get straight to the point. Today, I feel heavy. But not nearly as heavy as I did yesterday. I am referring to excess weight, but not the fat kind; the *heart* kind. I was feeling overwhelmed with obsessive thoughts about everything and everyone in my life that I can't control. Worry and fear and a healthy dose of self-pity were paralyzing me. I couldn't muster one positive thought or tap into even a tiny a nugget of hope. I read and prayed furiously, looking for something, *anything*, that might give me some relief from the despair that was consuming me.

Like I said, I am a bit lighter today. After a morning of asking God for help, He showed me, or reminded me, of a song. This memory was triggered by an entry by Sarah Young in my daily reading:

"God says to us, 'Hope in Me, and you will be protected from depression and self-pity. Hope is like a golden cord connecting you to heaven. The more you cling to this cord, the more I bear the weight of your burdens; thus, you are lightened. Heaviness is not of my kingdom. Cling to hope, and My rays of Light will reach you through the darkness.'"[48]

This message was sorely needed for me, but it's a message I know in my head already. It wasn't enough just to *know* the truth. I had to practice something different. And that "different" was revealed to me when I brought up the words to a song from my past, "Garments of Praise."

The chorus begins: "Put on the garment of praise, for the spirit of heaviness."

As I began to explore what that might mean for me, what promise I could cling to so I could lighten up, I began the process of shedding the weight. I thought about writing it down as soon as it occurred to me what I needed to do. But then, I decided to actually do it so I could give some evidence of success (clearly,

I still had my doubts about whether this simple plan would help at all). So what did I do? I stopped.

I stopped praying for God to help or fix all the things/people that I wanted Him to change/improve/empower, and I intentionally fixed my gaze on Him. I began by putting on the "Garments of Praise" song (Robin Marks) and sang with all my heart (the end of it has sort of an Irish jig feel, so you can even do a bit of Riverdancing/clogging if you're in decent shape!). The song has words that helped me express my desire to be comforted and refreshed and healed:

> Make these broken weary bones // Rise to dance again
>
> Wet this dry and thirsty land // With a river
>
> Lord our eyes are fixed on you
>
> We are waiting // For your garland of grace // As we praise your name [49]

But it's very hard to praise someone, namely God, when you are consumed with yourself. Throughout the Bible, praise is often associated with sacrifice. If that seems weird to you, let me explain. Psalm 116:17 says, "I will sacrifice a thank offering to you and call on the name of the Lord," and Hebrews 13:15 says, " … let us continually offer the sacrifice of praise to God, that is, the fruit of our lips, giving thanks to His name."

Many times, I don't feel like praising God because the pain or sorrow or hurt is so intense. These feelings require me to make a sacrifice. Sacrifice means that I do something I don't want to do or don't feel like doing. It's giving up my own desires for the benefit of someone else. And in this case, when I give God my sacrifice of praise, I choose to focus on two things:

1) His attributes. His power, love, compassion, grace, guidance, etc.
2) His track record. His history of how He has been good and faithful and shown up for me in countless, priceless ways. I believe that even if you are still skeptical of or even angry with God, you will have some stories to recount if you think hard enough.

I sacrificed what I felt like doing (worrying; fretting; trying to fix, manage, and control) and instead, fixed my mind, and voice, on who He is and what He has already done for me. It's the difference between listening to a sad breakup song about lost love versus a song expressing the power of love and the excitement and energy that comes from being in that relationship.

There are several ways to praise/worship God. I like to sing, so that's the main way that I engage in it. God doesn't really care if you can hold a pitch, though, so even if you can't, don't let that stop you! I also like to read various Psalms and adopt those words to help direct my thoughts.

If you aren't much for reading or singing, try writing down a gratitude list about who He is: all-powerful, all-knowing, all-seeing, kind, gracious, radical, extravagant. He is our rescuer, our provider, our savior, our voice of truth. Or maybe make a list of all the ways He has shown up for you in the past. Review the successes and times where you chose to trust and turn things over to Him. Note how much better they turned out than when you tried to depend on your own self-sufficiency.

I have been practicing a variety of all these since yesterday. Today is not perfect, but my heart is in better shape than it was yesterday. And for the record, nothing has changed in my circumstances. The adjustment has been where I am choosing to put my energy. Instead of wasting it on trying to control the uncontrollable (i.e. trying to do God's job for Him), I am making the sacrifice of praise in the ways laid out above.

In a society of chronic dieting, I think this might prove to be the best rapid "weight-loss" plan on the market. Care to trade a *garment of praise for that spirit of heaviness*? Could you stand to shed a few?

No more games

I am finally ready to admit it out loud: we are not a game-playing family. There. It's out there. For years we have tried to be game players. When my kids were younger, we really tried to make this a fun family activity, even though we knew from the get-go that it would ultimately end in crying and blaming and possibly throwing of tiny little game pieces--and that was just from the parents! As a whole, none of us gets any enjoyment from playing board games. For a few years we humored the grandparents and played games like Uno or Kings in the Corner, but even that has died out recently. I myself don't really hate cards, but you can only play so many games of solitaire. You really need more than one person to participate for any other type of game to be successful.

So, it's official. We don't like games. But I have to tell you that despite my disdain for games, I find myself inadvertently participating in certain games without even realizing I am playing. Usually it happens when I disagree with someone else's behavior or ideas or choices. Instead of letting them figure things out for themselves, I roll the dice when I stick my nose in their business and try to control or change the outcome. And even though I claim to be a "non-gamer," I try to impose my will on them and force them to play my game by my rules.

This is received with a resistance that is similar to what happens when I have tried to make my kids play board games when they'd rather be doing *anything* else. Then, and this is where the real danger comes in, there are the games I get sucked into playing by those who love to play certain kinds of games. When someone wants to argue with me or provoke me and get a reaction out of me, I often find myself playing with them, even after I have declared myself to be game-free. Here's what it looks like: Someone tries to engage me in something that really has nothing to do with me. Or they try to provoke me and get a reaction out of me or prove that I am wrong about something. I tell them I don't want to argue about it, but continue to engage, discuss it, or defend myself.

When I do this it's like telling someone I don't want to play catch. They ignore me and throw me the ball anyway. I catch it, throw it back, and repeat that I don't want to play their game. This continues over and over until I realize, I *am* playing. The only way to let them know I am not playing is to let the ball roll past me the next time they throw it. Just like you can't play tug-o-war unless you both pick up the rope, you can't have an argument unless more than one person is actively engaged in it. If I refuse to play, the game is over quickly.

Obviously, this doesn't mean you never have reasonable conversations or disagreements with people.

That's part of life. I am talking about the times where it is truly not even about you. Someone might be acting selfish, hateful, irrational, angry, resentful, stubborn, arrogant, or is affected by substances that could make a mature discussion impossible. You can choose not to play. You can detach with love, separating yourself emotionally and spiritually from the other person. You don't have to own their emotions or take responsibility for the fact that they have them (even if they insist you are the cause). And most importantly, you don't have to "win." Because you can't.

A helpful response that I have heard suggested is to pleasantly say, "You may be right," and walk away. That doesn't mean they *are* right or that you *think* they are, but it acknowledges that the feelings and thoughts they are having are real for them. It gives them dignity, and often, that is all they were looking for in the first place. I have also heard it said that "most people don't necessarily want to have their own way, they just want to have their own way *considered*."

You have most likely heard the words of the Serenity Prayer:

"God, grant me the serenity to accept the things I cannot change, the courage to change the things I can, and the wisdom to know the difference."[50]

In this case, the "things" we cannot change are other people and how they think or feel. The "thing" we can change is ourselves and whether or not we get involved in the unhealthy games that others try to rope us into playing.

God, today give us the courage to focus on ourselves and make the choice not to catch that ball or pick up that rope.

The secret

Almost 2,000 years ago, a guy named Paul said, "I have learned to be content whatever the circumstances. I know what it is to be in need, and I know what it is to have plenty. I have learned the secret of being content in any and every situation, whether well fed or hungry, whether in plenty or in want." Philippians 4:12

One might ask, how hard could his life have been in 62 AD? The guy wasn't married and didn't have kids (need I say more?). He wasn't slandered on social media or demeaned in the tabloids. However, a bit of history tells us he did endure a few minor inconveniences. During his short time of ministry, after God intervened and transformed him from a murderer to a missionary, he was flogged, imprisoned, beaten with rods, stoned, and shipwrecked (most of them on more than one occasion).

He was in danger from rivers, bandits, his own countrymen and religious leaders. He often went without food, sleep, water, and clothing. Oh, and then there's the anxiety from trying to spread the good news of God's love to a people whom he used to persecute and kill for believing that very thing. OK--I guess his trials and stressors might "win" over mine.

But somehow, Paul was able to find the secret to being content in all these circumstances. He credits two beliefs: 1) that he can do all things through Him, God, who gives him strength and, 2) he trusts that God will meet all his needs according to his glorious riches in Jesus. What amazing faith and assurance he had!

Still, I have to be honest with you about something. Even though I say I believe what Paul believes, those two "secrets" I mentioned above, I don't always live like I do. I don't act as if I really believe those words for myself. In fact, here's the reality of what I think much of the time:

I don't want God to take care of me so I can be OK no matter what my circumstances,

I want him to make my circumstances OK so I can easily take care of myself.

That's pretty embarrassing to say out loud. I really wish I was better than that. But my humanness and desire to be comfortable and happy and for everyone around me to behave and flourish, really gets in the way of trusting God no matter what--being content no matter what. It's scary when I realize that mostly I just want God to orchestrate my life so I don't need

Him so much. I mean, wouldn't that be easier for Him anyway? He has a lot of people to help, after all. Would it be so hard to just set me on a comfortable cruising speed and let me manage things myself?

Trying to wrap this up seems a little redundant. It's not like we haven't figured out what must be done. There is no new information. Life is good. And sometimes it's not. End of story. I can either complain about the times that are "not" or turn to God for strength to get through them, trusting that He will meet all my needs according to His glorious riches. I can forget about Him when circumstances are good or I can acknowledge that every good and perfect gift comes from God. I can choose to live with a grateful heart.

Whether my circumstances are pleasant or pressing, depending on God and staying in tight communication with Him are the only solutions that help me tap in to Paul's "secret" to contentment.

"Smells ring bells"

I just love the smell of a freshly lit cigarette in a hot car. Yes, really. It reminds me of when I was little and spent time with my grandma. I remember riding in her Cadillac in California while I jabbered and she smoked and listened. I actually have her piano in my house, which apparently, she antiqued herself, most likely while smoking. On hot, muggy days in Illinois,

I can sometimes smell hints of lingering smoke that must be mingled in with the paint. Neither of these are scents you would call pleasant or find as a featured fragrance at the Yankee Candle store, but for me, they trigger many emotions and happy memories of my grandma who has long since passed.

While doing some research to give validation to my personal connectedness with certain smells, I came across an article called "Smells Ring Bells ..." I was surprised to learn that "incoming smells are first processed by the olfactory bulb, which starts inside the nose and runs along the bottom of the brain … it has direct connection to two brain areas that are strongly implicated in emotion and memory. Interestingly, visual (sight), auditory (sound), and tactile (touch) information do not pass through these brain areas."[51]

So, apparently it wasn't unusual or weird that when I took a tour of my new work facility a few years ago, I started crying when I got to the wood-working shop (though the guy giving me the tour might have thought otherwise). My grandfather was a cabinet maker and when I was young, I spent a lot of time running around his shop, stirring up sawdust. Just getting a whiff of that scent took me back to those times and brought me to tears.

We all have them, the *smells that ring our bells.* But they are not always bells of celebration and joy. Sometimes, the bells they ring seem to be indicative of doom or mourning. I read of a war vet who had strong emotional and physical reactions to the smell of diesel from his time of active service. Haunting memories of death and tragedy flooded in.

Often the smells make little sense to anyone but us. Maybe it's the smell of a certain cologne that an abusive father, husband, or boyfriend wore that makes you freeze up inside. Or the stench of alcohol that takes you back to that scared little boy or girl who couldn't rouse their parent. Or the fresh smell of lilies that take you to the morning you stood beside your mother's casket.

You know the smells that trigger you. The emotions and memories, whether good or bad, can feel as real as the day they happened. This is good news and bad news, depending on the smell. Is it a sweet aroma or a stench? The feelings are very real, even if the events happened years before.

But it's important to remind yourself that *feelings aren't facts.* Acknowledging the feelings that knock on the door of your awareness is crucial. Let them in. Feel them fully. Accept them. Then let them go.

If the feelings are negative, remind yourself that they don't have power over you unless you dwell on them and let them tyrannize you. They are *feelings not facts.*

If the feelings are positive, remind yourself that those too are not facts. Enjoy the memories and special feelings but don't live there or pine to go back in time to "better days."

There are more scents on the horizon for you. Some will be lovely and some will stink like raw meat. Don't ignore how they make you feel but do remember to keep moving forward. Feel the feelings of the past but live in today. Be open to what God has for you in this present, real world.

FOCUS!

I have a lot to do today. A lot of odds and ends--phone calls and appointments to make, follow-ups on work and school activities, straightening after a weekend of ignoring household duties. All these duties are causing me to feel a bit flustered in my head and frozen on the couch, unable to sort everything out and make a go of any of it. From past experience (read: from doing it the wrong way over and over until I learned a bit of a lesson), I know that my day would continue on like this unless I pause and pray and "get God in there." So, I forced myself to pick up some books and start reading, getting out of my head and listening to what God might have to say to me.

I read a couple entries in my usual books and then one in a book I started reading again after a 14-year respite. It's called *Jesus, Life Coach* by Laurie Beth Jones. Every chapter starts off with the phrase, "With Jesus as your Life Coach you will ...." On this particular day's reading it said that I would "Keep My Focus." Well, that would certainly be helpful on this fine, snowy, scatter-brained Monday morning. Jones is a motivational writer and speaker, so her main point is about finding that one thing that keeps you going and eliminating all distractions that prevent you from staying on task and being successful. She uses Jesus' laser-like focus on His mission, ya know, to save the planet, as motivation for us to also stay focused on what we are called to do or be in this life.

I am not arguing with her, since most organizations sink or swim based on knowing what their *one thing* is. But as a woman who is, at best, average at most endeavors, I have always struggled to identify my *one thing*. I am the quintessential "jack of all trades, master of none."

But then ...

I moved on to my next reading by author Sarah Young, who writes using God's words to us from scripture. And, *I kid you not,* this was her opening sentence for January 29th: "KEEP YOUR FOCUS ON ME (caps all hers) ... let the goal of this day be to bring every thought captive to me ... I will guard you and keep you in constant peace as you focus your mind on me."[52]

Bless God's heart. He knows I don't have it in me to read between the lines today. He had to repeat

Himself *and* capitalize it. Lucky for me, and maybe you, I didn't miss the point. At least this was the point I believe He was making for me: *His will for me and for my life IS the "one thing." It overrides every other venture, goal, or practice.*

Think back on your life thus far. You have gone down multiple paths that took large amounts of your time and energy and passion. Most of them were probably very good things. But we are, by nature, continuously changing and morphing. What used to light your fire just doesn't do it for you anymore. That's OK. It's meant to be that way. So to hang your sign on any one door is unreasonable. There's an ebb and flow to life that needs to be leaned into.

There is only *one* constant. One overarching awareness that must influence our every thought: God's will for us and the power to carry that out. It must infiltrate every nook and cranny of our lives. Sometimes we have to discern His will for us in some pretty serious ways. But what I have found is that most days I just have to live out His will for me in all the tiny, seemingly insignificant encounters of my day. How did I react to the snippy sales clerk? Did I let that rude driver steal my serenity? Did my car breaking down cause me to question God's love for me? And what about in our relationships? Did I respond with compassion toward my discouraged teenager? Did I reach out to the friend who lost her job? Her husband? Her identity? Did I make a phone call to someone I know who is depressed or discouraged?

In the midst of all my muddled striving to make a big difference in this world, my consistent focus on God and seeking His will for me must be crystal clear. What I accomplish in this world is significant, but also temporary and fleeting. My primary purpose, my *one thing,* is to let God's will for me totally dominate (rule, govern, direct, be in the driver's seat, be at the helm of, rule the roost, wear the pants).

Turbo resentments

I am a spontaneous person. That is sometimes good. Sometimes not so good. When I write, it is a little of both. As a general rule, I sit on my couch in the morning, praying and reading and listening to what God is directing me to write about. It is usually more than obvious. Once in a while I have ideas as I am going through the rest of my day. I have a notebook that I grab and jot down the basics and save it for a future date. Then, when I experience that topic in some way, I go to my notes, pull it up and expand on it. Today is one of those days. My notes were written down awhile ago, but yesterday, a conversation with a friend brought it to my mind so I feel like the time has come to put it on "paper." I am pretty sure it's just a coincidence that most of the topics I have "saved for a later date" are ones that involve embarrassing stories about how I think or what I have said or done in the past …

It will come as no surprise to you that I struggle on occasion with resentments and forgiveness. I may have mentioned it once or twice in previous blogs. But about a month ago, I discovered a special, new kind of resentment. I have even coined a name for it: Turbo Resentment. Let me tell you about how I realized I harbored a couple of them.

I am a Realtor, so I was driving through a small town showing houses. There happen to be a few people from this town whom I have felt especially hurt and betrayed by. I have done quite a bit of work to forgive them and release my anger regarding the events that happened. I truly thought I was doing OK with this. I hadn't thought about any of it for a long time, until I drove through their town. Near their houses. Past places we used to go together. It all came flooding in and I had this very rational thought: "I hate this town." Yep. The whole town. I pray you don't live there. I was ready to write off the whole community based on the pain I felt just driving through it. I called my husband, because even though I felt wound up, I also found it semi-comical that I was holding on to so much unforgiveness that I was incorporating an entire town in the offenses. I told him about how I was feeling and that I was aware it was pretty messed up. And then, I saw the car. There is a certain car that one of those offenders drives that when I see one, I think, "I truly hate red Hyundais" (that's actually the kind of car I drive--the name of the actual car has been changed for obvious reasons). I called my husband back and told him that by the way, I also hate this type of car. He told me that I may have a problem. I concur.

These are a couple examples of Turbo Resentments. Do you have any of your own, or am I the only weirdo out there? Have you ever avoided a restaurant because that's where so-and-so works or where you used to go together before they hurt you? So much of what we experience is bound up in other people. Either good memories or bad ones can be connected to everyday objects, sounds, or smells. Do you feel angry when you hear that certain song, reminding you of how a relationship that was significant ended in betrayal? Do you hate a particular cologne or perfume because a friend who became your enemy wore it? Do you transfer your disgust to perfect strangers when they exhibit the same character defects as your ex?

Our strong and usually unreasonable reaction to neutral people, places, and things is a sign that we might not be as "free" as we thought we were. Maybe we only think we have forgiven because we aren't in regular contact with them. We think we are fine until we start sweating and feel our heart rate rise when we are triggered by something random that takes us back to the source of the pain. We realize there are clearly remnants, the sludge of the grudge, lurking in our hearts. Even though you and I don't recognize it on a regular basis, it affects our serenity. Our ability to be free. To move forward in peace with ourselves and with others.

I have said this before but it bears repeating: "Forgiveness is no favor. We do it for no one but ourselves." If we want to be free of bitterness and underlying anger, we have to forgive fully.

Root it all out. I truly believe that it is not an option to hate people. It is a complete anti-God state of mind. I never allow my kids to say hate about anyone. I barely let them say it about food or the like. That's how much I hate the word hate. But, somehow I have let myself off the hook about hating towns and cars. That somehow seems acceptable. But let's face it, we all know it's just a cover up for hating the actual people. It's just not OK with me to hate people, so I hate where they live and what they drive instead. Somehow, I don't think God sees them as all that different, and my heart still suffers from the same angst.

Living with resentments is hard enough. Harmful enough. Detrimental enough. But if you aren't feeling the freedom that comes with forgiving those you feel hurt by, maybe you are nursing some Turbo Resentments. Take a look at that today. Maybe it's never occurred to you that you are still in bondage to them.

Don't hate me (or my city or my car) for bringing this to your attention. ☺

What's NOT on your calendar?

Believe it or not, I am not too old to remember myself as a college freshman. I remember that I was very young, very naive, very excited, not always *right* but always *certain*. My passion and zest for life combined with a lot of new information and education (at a Bible college) was, on occasion, a recipe for a smidge of "know-it-all-ism." But I'll come back to that in a few paragraphs. I revered my professors and consumed books they recommended with fervor and an open spirit, ready to put into practice anything they suggested that sounded reasonable.

In one of my classes, we were assigned a book about how to manage your inner and outer world. Not only how to keep track of and stay in control of your daily schedule, but how *what* you did each day reflected *who* you were; what your outsides were saying about your insides. That's the gist of it. I admired the author and took his suggestions to heart, applying and reflecting on the principles he outlined for a successful Christian life, marked by integrity and discipline.

Think of my shock and disappointment when, not long after we read this book for that class, it came to light that this author had been caught in an extramarital affair. You can probably imagine the conversation among freshman Bible college students who, for all practical purposes, know very little about "real life" yet. We *thought* we knew an awful lot though, and judged others accordingly. There was no understanding or compassion for that author and, due to the nature of his book topic, he set himself up to be mocked accordingly: "So, what did his daily planner look like: 9:00 meeting, 10:00 Bible reading, 11:30 adulterous rendezvous, 1:00 lunch etc.?" We just couldn't wrap our minds around how such duplicitousness was possible.

Fast forward 29 years. I feel like I should make a formal apology. Not because what he did was OK. But because I have seen countless times in my own life where I lived in that same duplicity. Times when I claimed, and even believed, I was walking in the light of God's will but was simultaneously living in flat-out sin. Sometimes it was in obvious ways. Other times it was in less discernible ways, but still a blatant refusal to live an "inner life that matched my outer."

Let's look at it like this: I think that author, who challenged readers to ask themselves, "What's on my calendar?" might have been better off asking, "What's *not* on my calendar?" And I think we might be better off asking the same. Maybe you can relate to what I am saying better if I use a food analogy. Whether you have dieted or not, you have probably heard that a common suggestion for people trying to lose weight is that they write down everything they eat during the day. *Everything.*

The obvious goal is that this method will prevent you from eating junk because you know you will have to write it down and the shame of having to do that will cause you to eat fruits and vegetables instead. But the fatal flaw of human nature is that we are sneaky little things and we tend to find a loophole. When someone *does* snarf on a Twinkie or eat half a bag of chips, they conveniently forget to write that down. Even when meals are planned out ahead of time, which is often suggested, rarely does someone cheating on a diet go back later and fill in the gaps with 2 Cadbury cream eggs, 11 french fries, and a glass of wine.

The point is, maybe we should train ourselves to look regularly at what's *not* on our calendar. What are the subtle ways that, in hindsight, we are undermining how we say we want to live and what we say we believe about how to go about doing so. It's easy enough to review our day in big picture mode. But that doesn't always highlight the details--what's in the background.

Recently, I have been working on Step 10 of a Recovery program. The principle is one I think anyone could learn from: "We continued to take personal inventory and when we were wrong, promptly admitted it."[53] A quote from a reading on this step points out that "the wise have always known that no one can make much of his life until self-searching becomes a regular habit, until he is able to admit and accept what he finds, and until he patiently and persistently tries to correct what is wrong."[52]

We could prevent much suffering and heartache for ourselves and those we love if we would make a habit of this daily reading between the lines. What happened in the gaps, when no one was looking?

Perhaps we should look for areas where we have been self-centered, jealous, prideful, judgmental, angry, vindictive, braggadocious, sharp-tongued, arrogant, unforgiving, fearful, short-tempered, or lustful. Any of these, in word or deed, are deadly. They may not kill you immediately, but over time, if they go unchecked, they will lead you to those dark, secret places that you would never write down in your Day-Timer or schedule as a reminder on your mobile device.

Please hear me on this. This is an opportunity for you to be honest with yourself for the sake of growth and guarding your heart. Looking back on your day can help you identify areas in which you strayed from what you know to be true of who you are or want to be in your soul of souls, it is not a time set aside for self-flogging.

But hear me on this as well: if you ignore the maintenance of your soul, the rot will come. The axiom of the "slow fade" is tried and true.

That author did not set out to deceive his readers. He simply ignored and avoided a regular review of the subtle seeds of envy (of someone else's life, or wife), pride (I am above that sort of thing), and lust (meeting legitimate needs in illegitimate ways). Most people don't set out to steal money from their employer (it started with fear, selfishness, and greed that went unchecked for too long) or physically harm or kill another person (festering rage and unresolved resentments grew too big for them to contain). You get the idea.

"Act as if"

"Easier said than done," or in my case, "easier blogged than believed." It's ever so much easier for me to write about wise ways to live than it is to actually live them out in my daily life. The other day my son came into the room while I was working and asked what I was doing. I told him I was editing my book to get it ready for publication. His response? "*You're* writing a book?" I told him that indeed I was and that maybe he should read a few of my blogs sometime. His next response? "I don't need to read it. I *live* it." I suggested that he go ahead and read it because my blogging self is much wiser and more put-together than the mom sitting before him.

In any case, I am embarrassed to admit how different my written responses and my natural life responses can be. Today I am choosing to do it differently. I caught myself early in the day so, thankfully, I just might be able to have a day that I don't end up regretting by bedtime. I found myself anxious and worried about a variety of things that are not going my way (translation: things are not going the way I think they should go for those around me). I don't understand decisions or actions that have affected or been made by people I love. And to be honest, I am sort of honked-off about it. Well, at first I was sad. I cried a little and did a lot of whimpering and whining in God's direction (I'll get to the part about how I am doing it differently in a minute).

I'd been planning to write this morning, so this was really throwing a wrench in my plan for a lighter subject. But as usual, God uses my poor reactions and bratty behavior to help other people either avoid it for themselves or help them realize "they're not the only one."

So, to get to the point of how I am choosing to do it differently …

I choose to "act as if." I will "act as if" I actually trust God and His plan--His plan for me and for those I love, and even for those I don't like very much. I used to think that meant I was being inauthentic or fake. But I have come to understand it as a gesture of gratitude and trust--an acknowledgement of the track record that God and I have developed. One in which He actually *does* take care of me. Every. Single. Time.

I can write/say that I trust that God knows the big picture and has a plan that is bigger than the details of my life. I can write/say that sometimes difficult circumstances and disappointments can lead me to maturity and growth that can be experienced in no other way. I can write/say that I can live with a sense of joy and serenity, even when my life doesn't look like what I wish it looked like. I can write/say that I don't have to be in control of everything and everyone in order to feel secure. But … when push comes to shove, I have to confess to you that I have spent many a day tangled up in knots of fear, worry, anxiety, and despair. I forget to "act as if" all my words, whether written or spoken, are actually true.

As I said, today I choose to try a different route. One that might lead me to the peace that passes understanding. And if I practice "acting as if" often enough, it will bridge the gap between how I want to live and how I actually live. And maybe I won't have to "act" anymore.

The "good mood of the soul"

I really wanted to write about sleep this morning. Probably because "spring forward" was four days ago and I am extra-tired from waking up in darkness and lying awake, unable to get to sleep at my normal bedtime. However, as I started reading this morning, I noticed a recurring theme running through each author's insights: joy. So, as it goes in so much of life, sleep will have to wait.

I love how Methodist pastor Anne Robertson explains joy. She says that ancient Greeks described joy (*chairo*, in Greek) as "the good mood of the soul."[54] What a full description for such an indescribable sense of being. It's not a feeling, stirred by kind circumstances and memorable and cherished events. Joy, unlike happiness, can be a state we live in even when actual happiness is impossible. Brenè Brown says, "I'd like to experience more happiness, but I want to *live* from a place of gratitude and joy."[55]

And that seems to be one of the key ingredients to living a life marked by joy: gratitude. I realize this sounds simplistic, but when we keep in mind that "it could be worse," we will alleviate much of the complaining we do about our current circumstances.

When we choose to focus on the good in our lives, or even the absence of the bad, we are choosing to live in joy. We don't have to think very long, to come up with people we know who live in or have lived through horrific circumstances and tragedies with an aura of joy radiating from their spirit.

Nor do we have to think too hard to bring to mind someone we know who lives in a constant state of ingratitude and joylessness, even as they float through circumstances most people would envy. It's about attitude and gratitude. It's about perspective and choosing to see through the lenses that God prescribes, rather than our own smudged, scratched, and smeared pair of glasses.

Only with God's vision can we see clearly and face the endless flow of problems of this life with good cheer. In His presence we have a joy--a peaceful and restful state of soul and spirit--that no one can take from us (John 16:22) and that no turn of events can threaten.

Joy, it seems, is found most commonly in, well, the common. I remember very clearly my first "outing" when I was finally released to be out in public after my leukemia treatments. I had been neutropenic (having no immune system and susceptible to any and every disease) for weeks and was finally free to leave my house. I went to Hy-Vee. To a grocery store. And I could not have been more grateful. I was overwhelmed with joy. I had a deep appreciation for the very activity I used to dread--grocery shopping.

What had previously been drudgery was now a luxury. My perspective had changed. I was fully present and engaged in my day-to-day, mundane life because I had been rescued from death's doorstep.

Now ... I was lucky. Because it is far easier to have this amazing perspective when you have been taken to the edge of actual death. But it can still be done. And I highly recommend that you learn it today by choice, rather than having to learn it in the pressure-cooker of heartache, tragedy, or pain.

If we seek joy in the small gifts of everyday living --the tucking-in of a child, the observation of nature, the delightful taste of a well-prepared meal, the aroma of coffee in the morning, the fact that you can drink and bathe with running water, and the thousands of tiny blessings we take for granted--we might actually obtain it.

Happiness is fleeting. It comes and goes with the wind. But joy doesn't have to be. It can be your underlying "constant." The stillness of soul that comes from a heart bent toward unconditional gratitude. Without joy, we live deflated and defeated. We pump ourselves up with activity and vacations and entertainment and accomplishments, but when those things wane or falter, we are left lifeless and flat. Our remedy, our prescription for living in joy, is gratitude.

"Joy is what happens to us when we allow ourselves to recognize how good things really are."[56]

—MARIANNE WILLIAMSON

"I'll be peace"

In the '90s there was a movie that came out called *What About Bob?* Anyone seen it? I saw it approximately five times at the dollar theatre when I was in college. And I have probably seen it at least five more times at home and with my kids since then. One of my favorite scenes is when the psychiatrist (played by Richard Dreyfuss) comes raging into his 10-yr-old son's bedroom where he and Bob (a patient of his played by Bill Murray) are laughing and rough housing. He yells at them, "I want some peace and quiet!" At first they freeze, stifling their giggles, and then one of them says, "OK, I'll be quiet." And the other, with a smirk, says, "I'll be peace." ☺

I was remembering this scene as I was reflecting on the longing I have for peace. I want to "be peace" too. Naturally, I had to look it up, and my favorite definition is "freedom from disturbance; quiet and tranquility." (Merriam-Webster Dictionary). The reason I was ruminating on the idea of peace was because the last several entries I have read in my daily reading all mentioned it repeatedly. Apparently, I am not the only one who wants/needs peace.

I do think, though, that I may desire it at an unreasonable level. I mean, there is no end to the list of areas in which I wish peace could reign. I want peace in my heart and head (peace of mind, serenity of spirit). I want peace within my home (among my children,

God help us, and my spouse). I want peace with my friends, my clients, my co-workers, store clerks, and fellow drivers. I also want all of those same people to have peace with each other. And for my kids to have peace with all their classmates. I want peace between God and me and I want everyone I know and everyone they know to also have peace with God. Do you think I am being unrealistic? Maybe just a touch.

But honestly, I don't think I am alone in my wishing for peace. In fact, that seems to be the dominating desire of God's heart as well. If you recall, the greatest commandment in the Old and New Testament is "Love God. Love People." Love is at the very root of peace. God sent Jesus to this world to live and to die so that we can finally be at peace with God Himself. Jesus made it possible for us to be one with God again, taking on Himself the sin that once separated us. Freeing us to live in harmony with God.

You may have heard someone point out that the words "do not fear" appear 365 times in the Bible. Once for every day of the calendar year. It doesn't sound as cool, but the word "peace" actually appears approximately 429 times. Once for every day of the year and then some. Why? Because I am not the only one obsessed with having, giving, promoting, organizing, and communicating the significance of living in peace. God definitely is. And this is just my opinion, so take what you like and leave the rest, but

I believe you can sum up the theme of the entire Bible with that one word. *Peace.*

God has put that same desire in us. Think of all we do to acquire peace. We pray and meditate. We too often medicate. We take vacations and get massages and take yoga classes. We pay psychologists and listen to speakers and pastors and podcasts. We read self-help books and Bibles and horoscopes. We even fight wars and sign treaties. Some of these things work for us and some don't. But our desire to be right, to be at peace, with ourselves and our neighbors and our God is something we were designed to want.

So I guess I don't have to feel bad for my preoccupation with peace. I think I am in good company. I realize I am barely scratching the surface of the fullness of this beautiful word. But I hope it prompts you to contemplate your level of peace (with yourself, others, and God) and what legitimate and illegitimate ways you have been trying to obtain it.

Peace out, my friend ✌(that's slang for "Grace and peace to you," for anyone over 40 or without teenaged children).

A wide-angle lens

Lately I have been reading books with various perspectives on prayer and meditation. As I say those words, my guess is that if you lean more towards unconventional spirituality, the word "prayer" makes you feel slightly uncomfortable and perhaps even a bit tempted to skip this reading. If your spiritual practices lend themselves toward organized religion and church attendance and you "do devotions" on a regular basis, the word "meditation" may set you on edge or cause you to feel unsettled about where I am going with this.

Everyone do some deep breathing and relax. You know by now that I am not in the business of freaking people out or pushing my own ideas on anyone (sadly, I haven't always been that way ☺). I simply want to share a recent "ah-ha!" moment I had regarding both of these concepts. A few scales of confusion regarding these vast, vague, and mysterious practices fell from my eyes, and I was able to get a clearer vision of what they look like when I integrate them into my daily life.

I am about to give you a snapshot of prayer and meditation that I hope helps you the way it has helped me to take a step closer to applying these practices with a bit more clarity than you had before.

Some of you might know that I am a Realtor (this is relevant, I promise ...). Because of this, I have learned how to take quality pictures of homes when I list them. At first, I had a fairly nice camera that I used with the lens that came with it. The problem was, it is very hard to take any kind of usable photo of a tiny bathroom. I could get a really good shot of the toilet or bathtub, but not both in the same photo. I was informed by my photographer friends that I needed to get a different lens. A *wide-angle* lens. This would allow me to stand in the same spot, with the same camera, but adjust the lens so I could pan out and get a broader perspective, capturing all the magnificence of the, um, bathroom.

In short, this is simply an illustration of prayer. Richard Rohr calls it "a positive widening of your lens for a better picture." It is an "alternative processing system." Somehow, many well-intentioned religious people have turned prayer into what Rohr describes as a "pious practice or exercise that you carried out with the same old mind and from your usual self-centered position…This practice was supposed to 'please' God somehow. God needed us to talk to Him, I guess. Prayer was something you did when you otherwise felt helpless."[57]

Prayer can be juxtaposed with the word meditation, both referring to an entirely different way of processing life. Prayer/meditation is a "lens," the "wide-angle lens" that helps us to see the bigger picture of an otherwise narrow view of circumstances. And instead of seeing people with our blurry, tainted, and self-absorbed lens, we can use prayer/meditation to see them through God's lens. One that takes into account that their immediate behavior may be the reaction to and consequence of deep-rooted resentments, abuses, and feelings of abandonment or loss.

These practices take work. It is no easy task to invite God to, as the hymn says, "be Thou our vision." Rohr says "it always takes a bit of time to widen the lens, and therefore the screen, of life. One goes through serious withdrawal pains for a while until the screen is widened to a high-definition screen."[58] Most of us pray about what we want for ourselves and what we want for others. It takes discipline and a conscious decision to "turn our will and our life over to the care of God"[59] and let *Him* decide. To let what He wants for us and what He wants for others be the guiding principle of prayer and meditation.

When we widen our lens, we can see the world more clearly because we are aware that God's lens is bigger and fuller and crisper than any prayer uttered from our limited, self-centered, ego-centric vantage point. Our perspective changes when we see through this lens of prayer and meditation.

Views that were otherwise confined to itty-bitty spaces become fully developed to display the "reality" of how God intends for us to see the world.

And you might also be interested to know that the real value of a camera is the lens. I recently purchased a lens for my son--who regularly sells old camera parts for new and better ones on eBay--that cost almost five times as much as the camera itself. Because it's the quality and scope of the lens that produces the best pictures, not the *camera* (anyone else feel like a cheap camera in need of an upgrade?).

We have been given the ability to connect with the God of the *universe* through the gift of prayer and of meditation, so that we can see and experience life with the mind and heart--and wide-angle lens--of the One who sees All, knows All, and is All.

Everybody just calm down...

I've been trying something new lately. In the morning, before I get out of bed, I put on a 6-10 minute meditation and spend some time getting mentally and spiritually prepared for the day (it doesn't hurt that I also get to lie there for an extra few minutes … I'm a mixed bag of motives). This morning, about a minute into this practice, my time was hijacked by a persistent cat trying to claw its way into my daughter's bedroom.

It was equivalent to a person knocking and knocking without pause. My cat, Sunny Day, is adorable and cuddly and extremely old and, this morning, very annoying. I tried to continue to focus on the words of the meditation and the music and allowing God's Spirit to enlighten me, but all I kept thinking was that I wanted to strangle my cat and scream at my daughter to just let her in already! Eventually I had to quit and go open the door. It felt useless to lie there and fight it. I gave up.

Instead, I went to my spot on the couch, in an upright position (curse you, Sunny Day!) to do some reading. As per usual, as I was reading Brené Brown, she just happened to be addressing the importance of cultivating calm and stillness of mind and heart--meditation. I think most of us can agree that there are great benefits of doing so. Having written a bit about just such a topic a few days ago, I was especially intrigued by something that she pointed out about one of our biggest obstacles to actually following through with this practice: fear.

She points out that *"if we stop long enough to create a quiet emotional clearing, the truth of our lives will invariably catch up with us. We convince ourselves that if we stay busy enough and keep moving, reality won't be able to keep up."*[60]

The truth is, even though I know the importance of quieting myself and being still before my God, the very idea of "creating an emotional clearing" for Him to speak or soothe gives me much anxiety.

In trying to incorporate a practice to help me be less anxious, I end up feeling restless and jumpy because I so do not like to be still. Why? Because I am afraid. Afraid of what He might say if we are alone together. Afraid He might tell me to "go" do something or "stop" doing something or worse, do "nothing." Just let Him take care of it and just chill out for a half-second.

I have a friend (and it's probably not you, but it might sound like you) who says that when she is home alone, she turns all the TVs on because she hates it when it's quiet. She can't handle it. She's terrified of silence. So as she cleans or works from room to room, her mind is consistently distracted and occupied with other people's problems, drama, or scandal. She can focus on someone else's junk and intentionally leave no "clearing" or space for silent reflection on her own life.

I can be guilty of that in my own ways. Endlessly searching for a decent song on the radio while driving to my next appointment, three minutes away. Lying in bed, scrolling through Netflix to find my next new series to occupy my mind until sleep comes. Scouring websites to find an essential oil that will help me lose post-cancer weight (there isn't one, btw . . .). You might be able to throw in a couple examples I haven't even thought of!

My point is this: do not be afraid. Do not be afraid to slow down. To get un-busy. To be alone. To be quiet in your own home, in your own head. In order to do this, it is imperative that you choose to believe that God loves you, knows you, and longs to just "be" there with you. God isn't waiting to get you alone so He can shame you or lecture you.

Most of us do that to ourselves pretty effectively when we slow down enough to reflect on our behavior or attitudes. But God is not like that. He is kind and gentle of heart. And though He may bring to mind a stronghold (some character defect that "holds you strong") that He wants to relieve you of, He is always gracious, generous, and forgiving. We don't have to be nervous about being alone with Him. You may very well hear a tender whisper telling you that you are OK just as you are. That who you are today is enough. That where you are today is exactly where He intends for you to be. Take it one moment at a time and He will be with you.

It occurs to me that most of my attempts at quiet reflection are similar to my time in bed this morning, with Sunny Day relentlessly pawing at my daughter's door. Life is distracting. As they say, "The struggle is real." We can't control whether random thoughts, unwelcome emotions, or self-accusations come pounding on the door of our mind when we try to shut them out. All we can do is keep getting back to the business of ignoring them and putting our energy into focusing on what we love, what we are grateful for, and that God hears and sees us. He cherishes us. In doing that, we let go of fear and embrace the "peace that passes understanding."

In Isaiah 30:15 God says to His people, "When you come to Me, you will find rest and safety. When you are quiet and trust Me, you will find strength." Remember that we are His people too.

Within reach

This one has been in my notebook as a possible blog for a few months. I can't write as fast as ideas come to my mind so I outline them and save them for a time when they can be discussed from personal experience. I think today is the day for this one …

Regardless of how old you are, I am sure you have seen or heard of *The Andy Griffith Show.* I watched it a bit when I was little, mostly with my grandma. It was either that or *Hollywood Squares.* There was a character on the show named Otis. He was the town drunk who spent regular time in the county jail. However, it wasn't until recently that someone pointed out to me that Otis also had keys to the county court house and keys to the jail cell. He would often lock himself in and then hang the keys outside the cell, within reach. Totally missed that as a 10-year-old. In one episode, he even brought a suit to the cell and hung it up before going on a bender that night. He would need it to get dressed for church in the morning.

I am sure you are way ahead of me, but I just love this visual of what it looks like to keep ourselves locked up! It seems absurd that someone would remain in jail even though the keys to get out are in plain sight and are easy to grab. But, embarrassingly, I do this all the time. I think I might be doing it today, which is why I need to finally write this out, reason it out with you all, and maybe have the guts to use the keys.

Sometimes my cell is a situation or a relationship. But more often than not, it's a mindset. A dark, dank, cold, and hopeless place that I am choosing to live in, even when I know there is light and hope on the other side of the bars. Why is that?

I think there are a couple pretty understandable reasons why I am often more comfortable being locked up (angry, resentful, destructive, distracted, immobilized, etc.) than exercising my right to get free.

The most consistent answer in my case is *fear*. At least when I am engaging in circumstances and emotions and relationships that I am familiar with, I know what to expect and there are few surprises. Even if I don't like where I am, I am comfortable with how to behave and react while I am there. To leave the confines of my cell, I am opening myself up to new challenges and feelings that I may not know how to handle. I don't seem to be able to put my trust in God to take care of me when the new and different and healthy come my way. So I leave the keys hanging.

But there's also a humiliating and ugly answer for staying locked up, and that is for *sympathy*. I want to feel sorry for myself and I want others to feel sorry for me too. I may have a number of solutions at my disposal, but I refuse to use them. I don't do the reading or make the phone call or take the action. Instead, I come up with 101 reasons why those things won't work. The reality is, I get something out of staying locked up. I can feel sad for myself and manipulate others into feeling sad for me also. It's self-pity in its most heinous form.

Does anyone else have experience with keeping themselves incarcerated?

I hate to admit this out loud, but I am becoming more and more aware that even though my default setting when I feel stuck or trapped in a situation, relationship, or mindset is to blame everyone or everything around me, the truth is that I am the one choosing to stay in the cell. The keys are there for the taking. It's no one else's fault but mine if I let them dangle.

I have a choice. I have the responsibility. I am the only one who can turn the key (get the help I need, call that friend, pray that prayer, share my story, apply those principles, take that action) and set myself free.

Are you a dead ball?

If you were to look at my life from the outside, it would be hard to make a case that I don't know how to play. In the past couple years I have traveled to Paris, Hawaii, California, Las Vegas, Missouri and Michigan (hey, it's not Illinois so those last two still count!). I have gone to concerts, sat poolside at friends' houses and made day trips to shop in St. Louis and Chicago. I've attended plays, laughed myself silly at a Seinfeld show and hosted numbers of girls-only patio parties and dinners around my dining room table. To an outsider, this might seem like evidence that I haven't forgotten everything about how to play.

And yet …

Playing is not just about being present ***at*** the activity, it's about being present ***in*** the activity. Big difference. I have been thinking about this word "in" and how it relates to play. My mind keeps going to baseball terminology. Even if you are not a baseball fan, you probably understand the basics enough to track with me for the next couple paragraphs.

Baseball is a game that people play (I know … profound insight, H). For the purpose of this blog, let's pretend you are the ball. I think it's fair to say that the ball is a crucial part of the baseball experience. But the ball has a job to do in order for the game to be played. It can't just lie on the pitching mound or in the dugout or sit in the 2nd baseman's mitt.

It has to be an active participant. The ball has to be "in play." If a player hits it outside the lines into foul territory, it is considered "out of play." Don't you just love it? What a perfect metaphor for how we must play! It's not enough to just show up for the activity. We have to be present and engaged in it. We have to be "in play," otherwise the game is not fun. It's not exciting. It's not fulfilling its purpose.

So much of the time, I am attending the game but I am not "in play." In Recovery, we remind ourselves to "keep our head with our hands." It means that we remind ourselves to keep our mind where our body is. To focus our attention and love and laughter on the current moment without letting our brain wander off, rehashing what happened yesterday or worrying about what will happen next week. I have participated in many "play-full" activities over the past few years, but too often have been *outwardly* present while *inwardly* "out of play."

It's not complicated. I can probably just shut up now. You get the gist. Again--being *at* vs. being *in* … Two tiny words. *At. In.* But whichever one you choose to embrace will either inhibit or enhance your ability to play.

One last thought on the baseball front …

You remember what they call a ball when it is "out of play," right? "***Dead.***"

But thank God, the opposite is also true.

Only when you are "in play" can you be "***live***" and get your game on.

Harmonious

I don't always do it or do it well, but the primary purpose of my life in a nutshell is to live out the suggested 11th Step of the 12 Step Recovery Model: seeking "through prayer and meditation to improve my conscious contact with God as I understand Him, praying only for His will for me and the power to carry that out."[61] Everything else I do, feel, or think falls under that umbrella. But how exactly do I determine what His will is? How do I differentiate His perfect will from my selfish will that I so often try to sneak in or disguise as something resembling God's will?

Maybe it's more simple than it seems. Is it possible that we have complicated it to the point where we don't even bother attempting to listen/learn/discern His will? That we just live out our own will, cross our fingers and pray that He blesses our activities and our loved ones?

Let me give you an analogy that might help you come to a clearer understanding of it. "It" being the massive and mysterious "Will of God" question, summed up by a goofy 47-year-old momma. Take it for what it's worth.

I sing at church on occasion. I have been singing since I was little, and since we're on the topic, let this serve as a formal apology to all my parents' house guests that I supposedly entertained with various vocal numbers in our living room during the '70s. ☺ I have been told I have a decent voice, but I have to admit something to you all: after years of experience I simply cannot pick out a harmony part (that's the complementary part sung with the melody that enhances the beauty of the sound, for those of you who don't speak music lingo …) to save my life.

When I sing at church I am usually assigned the harmony part and I have to practice it over and over and over before rehearsal. Because of this, I never forget that part. It is burned into my brain and I hear it in my sleep. But here's what I have noticed; any time I sing that song, even if I am singing alone, I am not really sure if I am singing the melody or the harmony part. And the harmony part sounds really dumb on its own, so you would think it would be obvious. But since I practiced and rehearsed it so many times, I literally can't tell the difference.

And that's how I better understand how my will and God's will are intertwined. If I am always seeking to improve my conscious contact with Him through prayer and meditation and, I might add, obedience and loving and serving others, then His will and mine will be lined up to the point that you can't tell the difference between them. The harmony and melody are in perfect play.

For me, this realization of living my life in God's good and perfect will, being in perfect tune with Him, means my prayers are different than they used to be. My expectations are different. Let's use work as an example. Instead of expecting God to show me the exact job I need, I seek Him first, make the best decision I can, and take Him with me wherever I go. If I am humble and available, He can work through me and my circumstances regardless of which job I choose.

If I hate that job, it doesn't mean that I picked wrong; it more likely means my attitude is off kilter. If I get fired or am abused at that job, I can use it as an opportunity to grow in faith and seek Him further as to what to do. So often we get down on ourselves, assuming we misunderstood Him. Or we did it wrong. Just because something doesn't go smoothly or is challenging doesn't mean it was a wrong decision. Remember, there are always other people and powers who are not seeking His will that conspire to fight our submission to it. Ask yourself what God has for you to learn in those times.

On some occasions, when things don't turn out as wonderful as I expected, I can sometimes trace it back to a point where it was obvious that something other than fulfilling God's will distracted me. The dollar signs. Potential accolades. The opportunity for power. The easier, softer way that threatens to weaken my character.

Jobs are just one of a thousand areas where discerning God's will can feel like an unsolvable mystery. We feel so small and powerless to make such life decisions. But we are not. The person who abides in God is in the will of God. God not only expects me to do His will, but His power resides in me to help me do it. If my relationship with Him is personal and I lay down my life before Him, I can trust that He will redirect me from the inside out if I wander off. Your conscience will lead you as God's will coincides with your will and becomes the tune in your ear that you cannot shake.

This analogy gives me a fresh understanding of a verse you may have heard before: Take delight in the Lord and he will give you the desires of your heart (Ps.37:4). In light of this goal of aligning my will with God's, I realized that this verse doesn't mean that God will give me whatever my heart desires as long as it is in line with His will, but rather that when I delight in Him (seek, serve, love, listen, and obey Him), my desires and His desires will become one and the same. Possibly, harmonious.

Rules are made to be broken

For some reason, while I was taking my in-laws to the airport last week, I made a comment about how I was a "rule follower." I was a little surprised that they seemed *very* surprised that I thought this about myself. They didn't share my assessment. It might have something to do with a couple maneuvers I made to get them to the airport on time, claiming that certain traffic laws were merely suggestions. At any rate, I guess I should explain that even though I may not agree with or follow certain rules, there are a couple rules I have about myself that I can't seem *not* to follow, even though they aren't necessarily based in reality or contribute to healthy, whole-hearted living.

Lately, I have been writing about finding my "skip" again. Learning how to "play" and live a lighthearted and joyful everyday life. I'd say I am making a little progress, in case you were wondering how it's going. But I realized that I have established a couple rules when it comes to my "play-time." When I keep these rules, I find it hard to truly engage, relax, and fully enjoy what I am doing and who I am doing it with.

One of the rules is for *me*, and I have mentioned it before. This rule tells me that I have to *earn the right* to play. It's the Cinderella syndrome: until I have scrubbed the floors, dusted, vacuumed, mowed, helped kids with homework, cooked dinner, sold three houses, and helped out at church, I can't go to the Ball. And if somehow I managed to get there, but hadn't finished all my tasks, I couldn't dare enjoy myself while I was there. I had to think about all that wasn't done yet and all I had yet to do. I had to hold on to the guilt of taking care of myself and letting some things go. I couldn't just admit that I simply can't keep the pace I have set for myself. I had to admit that I wasn't Wonder Woman and that once in awhile I just had to take a break and let my hair down, and no one was going to suffer. I don't know where I got this rule exactly. But I have been letting the rule *rule* me for far too long. It's time for an uprising.

The other rule I have is for *you*--for my friends, family, and people who I "play" with. This one can be illustrated with a real-life example from my past. Several, as in about 10-15 years ago, I organized a game to play with a group of our friends. I am from Napa, as many of you know, and this was a Napa Valley board game. I had purchased the wines from the wineries on the board that one might land on, as well as educational information about the wines that, naturally, they would want to learn about with acute attentiveness on a Friday night … with a large group of friends … while drinking wine. Needless to say, my expectations of the evening did not end up matching the reality of it. But boy, they were having a blast! They were not, however, cooperating with my rules about how they were supposed to be having this so called "fun." I remember being quite incensed. Wounded. Hurt. Taking it personally and pouting that they weren't "doing it right" (read: "doing it my way"). I didn't enjoy myself at all because they weren't playing by my rules.

When I follow such a rule, I give other people the power to ruin my day. To steal my joy, as I often put it. And, I might add, I will not be invited to many events that require a lighthearted, easy-going, relaxed presence. It hurts everyone when I try to control other people and dictate their manner of "fun-ness." No one can truly engage in life-giving play when Mrs. Bossy Pants is around. Especially me.

Since, at my core of cores, I don't really like rules, may I make a *suggestion*? Whatever rules you are following, that you have made up from the broken, wounded, controlling, fearful, anxious places in your soul, annul them today. Are they about how you give or are willing to receive love? How you speak to others and yourself? How you share? How you think about yourself, or God, or others? What you expect from your life and the people in it? Whatever rules you have been playing by, if they rob you of the ability to live peaceful, happy, and free, obliterate them. Declare them invalid.

THESE RULES WERE MADE TO BE BROKEN.

My cup runneth over (with what? is the question)

I am trying to come up with a clever way to start this entry without leading with something like, "In the 23rd Psalm it says ...." To some, Bible verses feel antiquated and childish. But I don't think I can do it. Just trust me that it will be relevant to your life and keep reading (pretty please).

So, in the 23rd Psalm, which most people have heard at least once in their lives (you know, "The Lord is my Shepherd …"), the end of verse 5 says "my cup runneth over." It's interesting to note that whatever "it" is in the cup, isn't just full to the brim, contained, and controlled, it is spilling out and overflowing. And who says that the stuff in the cup is liquid? Couldn't it also be overcrowded, bursting, busting at the seams, bulging, and jam-packed? At any rate, that sucker is not big enough to hold all that is continuously being poured or packed into it.

I am not going to pretend to provide an exegesis (fancy word for a critical and smart explanation of scripture) of this phrase, I am simply going to tell you the state of mind, torqued as it was, when I read "my cup runneth over" in a book about the 23rd Psalm. I was reading along and when I got to that verse, a voice in my spirit surprised me. The paraphrased version was: "Oh, it runneth over, all right! Overflowing with problems, frustrations, issues, questions, doubts, and irritating situations!"

Nice attitude, right?

There were, and are, some areas of my life (read: "areas of other people's lives whom I love and feel compelled to fix, manage, and control") that are challenging and disappointing (read: "not living up to my expectations or giving me warm fuzzy feelings"). I certainly felt that my cup "runneth over" beyond containment. My natural response was to complain to

God about this and demand, as nicely as possible, an explanation.

The other night, my husband and I were discussing Albert Camus' *The Myth of Sisyphus* (just some light marital bonding conversation ☺). You know, the story about the futility of life? Roll a giant bolder up a big mountain, only to stumble near the top, lose control, and have it roll back down. Over and over and over for as long as you live. This is Albert's analogy about our lot in life. Very inspiring, right? My two-cents' worth during our discussion was, yes, life is basically a lot of hard work and often very redundant; the only factor we really have control of is our choice in how we do it. Will we choose to whine and complain about the sweat and sore muscles, or will we whistle while we work?

I suppose my point is that on the off chance that you occasionally feel like your cup-o-crap is indeed running over (and over and over and over), you, like me, have a choice. Because there are also thousands upon thousands of reasons to see it with different eyes.

A gratitude list is one of the best ways to keep mindful of all the blessings (even when they are disguised as difficulties) in our lives, the lives of others, and in the world at large. Some days your list may only consist of your being thankful you didn't kill anyone that day. Hey, it's a start! But soon, I think you will find that you have to cut yourself off from writing down all that is "good" in your life because you run out of time.

Some days it might be the superficial stuff (coffee ice cream, Netflix, no humidity, Starbucks, a good parking space, a sale on those shoes you have been eyeing, etc.). Then there are the basic things we should be grateful for but sometimes take for granted (sleep, air, nature, healthy food, drinkable water, friends, family, etc.). It's that final level of gratitude that tells us where we are with God and whether or not we trust His ways in the world (grateful for this or that problem/situation/difficulty that produces perseverance, tenderness, tolerance, compassion, empathy, and a brave and determined spirit in us).

This morning, a reading from Oswald Chambers made me weep. Mostly because I so often think such inaccurate and flat-out wrong thoughts about God when I choose to believe that He has filled my cup with everything but the blessings. "There are times when God will appear like an unkind friend, but HE IS NOT; He will appear like an unnatural Father, BUT HE IS NOT; He will appear like an unjust judge, BUT HE IS NOT. Keep the notion of the mind of God behind all things strong and growing ... You can rest in perfect confidence in Him."[62] (Capitalization mine)

My sweet friend, does your cup, like mine, feel like it's overflowing with everything opposite of goodness and mercy? First of all, you are not alone. But it is vital for both of us to choose to trust God's bigger plan. His desires for us are immeasurable beyond all we could ask or even imagine. Start seeing with new eyes the layers upon layers of blessings that are there all the time if we choose to focus on them.

Grateful for air-conditioning

Maybe if I just start typing my brain will untangle itself about what I want to say today. God must be trying pretty hard to teach me about living in the moment, because my brain continues to circle back around to that lesson I have yet to learn, apparently. Or maybe He just knows that in most cases, I need lots of reminders.

This morning while driving my kids to school, I was chuckling to myself (since no students in my car are interested in hearing my insights before school or before 8:00 a.m.--go figure) about a conversation I had with my oldest son who is currently renting a room out in California. He doesn't want to commit to an apartment until he decides where he is going to land once he finds a job that can help him along in his career path. Unfortunately, California is running at about 110 degrees lately and since he is only renting a room, he has no control over the thermostat. And even more unfortunately, the person who does have control is the one who pays the bills and they seem to feel that 85 or 90 degrees is a reasonable temperature to keep the house. I say all that to tell you about my (in my head) response to all that: "I bet he wishes he had been more grateful for that annoying dorm life last year!" for the air-conditioning control privileges. If only he had known what was coming, he would have cranked it up to 72 and relished what he would one day long for as he lay dripping sweat in his bed (my poor baby!).

But isn't that how it works? We don't know what we've got 'til it's gone? I have lost track of how many times I have kicked myself for not wearing a bikini when I was 20 and size 4! I just couldn't enjoy my body because it wasn't "enough" of where I wanted it to be. Now I think, I should have been grateful that I looked the way I did instead of wishing I had "that girl's" body.

It gets more serious than fat vs. skinny, too. I remember wishing I had a bigger house or better car or job. And I am ashamed to admit that though I haven't wished for different kids or a different spouse, I have wished for a kid who minded better (when they were toddlers) or talked sooner (when they were babies) or did more or less of what our society deems successful and well-rounded. I have wished my husband was as attentive or romantic as men in movies who are paid to act that way or as financially successful as so-

and-so's husband. I am not proud of these thoughts. Mostly because it shouts that I am living in the past or the future. Regretting that I didn't embrace what I used to have or pining for what has not yet come.

Both of these states of mind keep me from being present. From being grateful for *this* day, *this* moment. This one and only precious life. If we can learn to say "thank you" to God, to ourselves and to those around us for contributing to where we are today, we can avoid living in the past or waiting for our lives to change so we can be happy. Today is all we've got. It's time to stop feeling sorry for what was or for what *isn't* and start being grateful for what *is*.

"Sick and tired ..."

Regardless of what you think of Bill Cosby, you have to admit that he has some pretty hilarious insights into parenting. When I was little we had a cassette tape of *Bill Cosby: Himself.* He did a little bit about how his mother was always "sick and tired" of this and "sick and tired" of that. And how *tired* always followed *sick*. He said, "Worst beating of my life, my mother said 'I am just sick ...' and I added ' ...and tired.'"[63] ☺

Well, I too am "sick and tired." I am sick and tired of waiting. Because even though waiting implies that one is inactive and biding one's time, it is actually much more involved and requires a lot of energy that

I don't always have. One definition of waiting is "to remain stationary in readiness or expectation." Another is "to look forward expectantly or hold back expectantly" (Merriam-Webster Dictionary). Did you catch the repetition of the word expectant? In other words, you are waiting *for* what is being waited *on*. You might be waiting for a train that is coming (looking forward expectantly) or waiting for a chance to strike (holding back expectantly). Either way you look at it, waiting is actually a pretty intentional and intense state of being.

You may be wondering what I am sick and tired of waiting for. On the surface, it has to do with the fact that for five whole days I have been exercising and watching what I eat and drink to the point of sacrifice--and I haven't shed one single, solitary pound. Some might argue that it isn't all about the weight. I had that argument as well. So I measured my arms, legs, belly, etc. Nope. Nada. Exactly the same. And sheesh, after five days, shouldn't there be some reward? But like I said, that's just the surface stuff. There are several other areas of my life that I am starting to get impatient about. My timing and God's timing just don't seem to be coinciding. Most likely because my timing is always "by the weekend."

As I mentioned, another component of waiting is the thing we are waiting for. Unfortunately, we usually have hopes and desires for what that will look like, but know that ultimately we can't control the outcome. At least when it comes to changing ourselves. All we can do is the footwork, the inner-self-soul-work and see what happens. Just because we read, pray, study, and practice living a spiritually and emotionally healthy lifestyle, it doesn't guarantee that the results will meet our expectations. Our marriage may not improve in the areas we want it to. Our friendships might need to be altered or abandoned. Our job might not be salvageable. Our kids may still rebel or refuse to reconcile with us. We simply can't control that "thing" that is being waited for, the results that are yet unrealized.

Boy. Now we are all super depressed. ☺

It's just a truth of life that "time takes time" and even as we wait for the fulfillment of that "time," we wait with expectation. It doesn't mean we need to stew and worry about what is to come; it means we do what we can and leave the results up to God. Trusting that His timing is perfect and remembering that there are other people in the world whose lives might depend on the timing of mine--(Imagine that! The world doesn't revolve around me?!?!)--are a couple of practices that bring me to a place of acceptance for where my life is today.

I don't have to *like* waiting for positive changes. But I can choose to live with a state of mind that accepts that time can't be rushed. That I have very little control over the exact results, but that I can continue to participate in the practices that might eventually bring about positive changes in my own little world.

Without the perspective that comes from trusting that a Power greater than ourselves (whom I call God) has a plan that weaves my little Heather-plans together with all of your plans to fulfill His plans, we will indeed be "sick and tired."

You are aware ... (or are you?)

I started off thinking I was going to talk about attitude adjustment. Not that I need one or anything. Just in case someone else might need one and hey, I'm here to serve. ☺ But as I did a few readings, I realized I need to back it up a bit and talk about the first step in adjusting an attitude: *awareness.* It's been awhile since I read the way I used to, where I read three dated entries from three different books. Today I decided to do that and as you can probably guess, the word *aware/awareness* literally popped up in every single one. It makes me smile when God makes the message so obvious. He must've known I needed extra assistance today ...

AWARENESS: That's the word of the day. Write it down and then ask yourself, or a few friends, family members, or co-workers, "How *aware* are you?" Are you aware of the areas of your character, your behavior, your perspective on your circumstances that need attention? Would you or those you ask say that maybe, just maybe, there are one or two things about your attitude that could use some tweaking?

Until we are aware of what needs to change in us, there will be no growth. Becoming aware isn't easy.

The best, or at least the most preferred and softest way, to spur change is through a gentle whisper or nudge from God to pursue it. Sometimes that is called feeling "convicted." God has some work to do on you and He has let you know in a way you are ready to accept and spend time working on.

But alas, most of us have to come to this awareness by being jolted out of our ignorant stupor by something akin to being hit by a Mack truck. We are going along, feeling like we are pretty awesome, when a spouse, a child, a friend, or mentor expresses concern or displeasure about a particular character defect in us. It stings and we are wounded at first, then angry and defensive, but in the end are at least willing to entertain the possibility that we aren't as awesome as we thought. The process of rooting out, fine tuning, and tweaking our weaknesses begins.

Probably the most effective and horrific way we become aware of our messed-up selves is through an enemy. This just makes my skin crawl. It's excruciating to be sent truth through the mouth of someone who doesn't love us or want the best for us. Their goal is to hurt or maim, but if we are able to ask ourselves the hard question, "Is there any truth to what they are saying about me?" we might see, or become aware, that our selfishness, arrogance, impatience, abruptness, indifference, or thoughtless words were part of what sculpted this enemy.

Sometimes when I read over past blog posts or a few chapters of my book, I see strong, repeated patterns regarding worry, fear, control,and judgmentalism. I think, "What is *wrong* with me that I don't seem to be able to apply the truths I write about and get better once and for all!?" I am a work-in-progress for sure. But without being confronted with the hard circumstances of betrayal, addiction, cancer, and other challenges that have come my way over the past few years, I don't think I would even be aware that those demons were lurking inside me. And without *awareness* there is no hope of transformation. And even though change is hard, and often slow, I would rather be aware of where my life-attitudes need adjustment than to be clueless, ignorant, and in denial.

All this change and growth takes time. And usually the changes and growth are tiny and subtle. But as my Recovery book says, "Gradually, and at first imperceptibly, our outlook (attitude) shifts." But time is a gift. "Time offers me evidence" that what I am doing is working. This evidence of changed behavior over time, provides reinforcement and "strong support in times of doubt and helps boost my courage in times of fear."[64]

It gave me chills when, reading with great anticipation, I came across the word "awareness" in my September 18th entry of *Jesus Calling.* I knew immediately that this line was offering the principle that makes all of the above possible. Author Sarah Young uses Jesus' words in scripture to say, "It is so important to stay in communication with Me, living in thankful awareness of My Presence."[65] Without a dependent and grateful relationship with a Being who can do miracles, *even in me*, I will just be spinning my wheels and remain indefinitely stuck in my oblivion.

Down to go up

My brain is hurting a little. I have been reading (and I am still in the introduction after a couple of weeks) a book called *Falling Upward: A Spirituality for the Two Halves of Life.* It makes perfect sense and at the same time is really hard to explain. The concept is profoundly simple, but it is stretching my mind to figure out how to narrow down such a huge concept into 500 words or less. I'll try to summarize it and then I suggest you just go buy the book.

The author, Richard Rohr, a Franciscan priest, poses the possibility that there are two halves of life, and that the second half comes when we move from surviving to thriving. It doesn't mean that it will happen exactly halfway through our lifetime, obviously.

In "Richard Rohr for Dummies" lingo (since this is the only way I know to explain or understand him), it means that the thriving part of life comes after we play the first half of the survival game, regroup, refocus, and refresh during a symbolic "half-time," and then burst out, guns blazing, into the second half.

It's during this second-half living that we discover "the task within the task," or what Rohr calls "what we are doing when we are doing what we are doing."[66] Life becomes more acutely about the *how* than the *what*. How we go about our daily duties and fulfill our responsibilities. Are we focused on the results more than the integrity of how we get there?

If so, we are still stuck in first-half living--mere survival. As Rohr puts it, "Integrity largely has to do with purifying our intentions and a growing honesty about our actual motives. It is hard work. Most often we don't pay attention to that inner task until we have had some kind of fall or failure in our *outer* tasks."[67] In laymen's terms, "Ya gotta go down to go up."

Ugh. I don't like that. And I suspect I have lost a few of you as well. Many of us want to live with this "second-half" mindset, but at the same time, also want comfortable habits, a steady income, and stress/problem-free lives. If getting to this second-half living is a result of being purified and strengthened through trials, we'd rather stay in the locker room, thank you very much.

Well, fortunately or unfortunately, we don't usually have a choice in the matter. Some kind of falling, what Rohr calls a "necessary suffering," is programmed into the journey. It's not that suffering or failure might happen, it's that it will happen, and to you! These are all part of the human journey whether we like it or not. The question for each of us is how we choose to react to it.

Will we dig our heels in, straining to maintain life as we have always done it--desperate to fight it off or avoid rocking the boat we have been sailing for the first half of our lives?

Or do we choose to embrace the opportunity to embark on a new adventure? An expedition of uncharted territory? We fall into this new way of living. You have to go down to go up, as they say. But it's worth the risk.

I know this. Because I have done it. Or it has been *done* unto me (not to be confused with being done to me). I have been faced with many sorrows, betrayals, upheavals, and the literal threat of death itself. Am I different as a result? You bet your bippy I am. But I am not just different, I am new. I still struggle with many of the same character defects, but today I have perspective and new tools to approach the second half of my life with a new pair of glasses. The "lenses" through which I view life have been drastically altered. And as much as I hate to say it out loud, I know that I know that I know that it has only come as a result of suffering. I am who I am because of what I have had to dredge through. And even though I don't wish it to come again, I also don't resent or regret any of it.

It has made me who I am today and most of the time, I kinda like the new me.

(Dangit--that was 726 words.)

Pull yourself together!

"Pour yourself a glass of wine, put on some lipstick and pull yourself together."
-Elizabeth Taylor

Recently a friend gave me an adorable makeup pouch with this quote on it. I do wholeheartedly agree that lipstick is the cornerstone of all cosmetic collections, but that's neither here nor there. There's been some wildness going on in my head and heart lately, and today, as I admitted to God that I felt like I was going insane, He narrowed the tornado in my head down to the eye and in one word revealed the problem: *control* (or lack thereof).

You see, I have this chronic disease of trying to control; of trying to make people, places, and things around me OK so I can be OK. This approach leaves very little time and energy to enjoy my own life and explore what God has designed me to be and instead keeps me focused on, and actually obsessed with, the behavior, choices, lifestyle, successes, failures, problems, disappointments, and fears of people around me. Usually the ones I love the most. The problem is two-fold, however. I am not the only one who suffers in this scenario. No one likes to feel that they are responsible for someone else's well-being. And no one likes to be told--or as I like to say "encouraged"--to live their life according to someone else's plan. As a result, they end up feeling resentful and disrespected and certainly *not* loved.

After I prayed (more like "cried out" or "vented") about how I felt like I was going crazy and simply could not handle all the problems and challenges my loved ones are facing, God finally showed up. Or should I say, I finally hit my bottom and surrendered, admitting that my way wasn't working and He could finally get a word in … yeah, maybe that's more like it. A few quotes from my Recovery reading for today that helped me see clearly why my peace of mind had blown clean away:

"Surrender does not mean submission - it means I'm willing to stop fighting reality, to stop trying to do God's part, and to do my own."

"The best way I've found to invite serenity is to recognize that the world is in good hands."

"Today I can be grateful that the earth will continue to revolve without any help from me. I am free to live my own life, safe in the knowledge that a Higher Power is taking care of the world, my loved ones and myself."

"There is only one person I am responsible for, and that is me. There is only one person who can make my life as full as possible--that too, is me ....Today I will keep hands off and keep my focus where it belongs, on me."

-ALL QUOTES[68]

After I went to the index and read every single reading on surrender and control (about 10 readings--apparently other people struggle with this same disease), I had clarity for the first time in a long time. At the bottom of the page for today's reading I wrote, "It feels irresponsible to enjoy my life unless my loved ones are enjoying theirs." This belief is one I need to kick out if I am ever to embrace and find joy in my one and only life.

I have to remember that God doesn't have grandkids, He just has kids. And when I try to impose my will on others, either directly by offering advice they didn't ask for or indirectly (by praying to God that He do with them what I want done), then I am interfering with His perfect plan for them and missing out on His beautiful, exhilarating, and personal plan for me.

It shouldn't surprise me that when I went to my reading for today in *My Utmost for His Highest,* Oswald Chambers titled today's entry, "Pull Yourself Together."[69]- He wrote that in 1935, waaaaay before Elizabeth Taylor. His point was basically, "God is God and you are not." And He's "got this."

Jedi-mind treatment

The other day, after trying to talk both of us off the ledge of a particularly frustrating situation, my husband asked me, "Why do you always see the bright side?" That's when I had to confess that even though I had just rattled off a bunch of "bright side" jargon, I actually woke up on the Dark Side that very morning. After a few decades, I have finally learned that when I am disturbed, short-tempered, or enraged at minor inconveniences, things that don't go my way or say, heavy objects falling off the table directly on my big toe, it's a pretty strong sign that there is something boiling inside me (and it's probably been percolating for an unrecognized while).

What is even more disturbing is how quickly my mood, my outlook on my circumstances can vacillate from one end of the continuum to the other. That morning, I was having a toddler-esque tantrum over some pretty lame stuff, which triggered me to go on a rant to God about how my life was a joke and nothing ever goes my way and why does everyone else seem to get what they want but I certainly never do!?!?!

I knew even as I was driving that I was setting myself up to feel stupid for my lack of perspective. You see, I was driving to a hearing for a young man who has been in jail--has not seen the literal light of day --for a year. The lesson I was about to be served hung out there, taunting me, but I still couldn't manage to pull myself together. I just kept mouthing off, right up to the point where I put my two quarters into the parking meter for the guy parked behind me! Just one more bit of evidence that my life was indeed jinxed by God (thinking about this in hindsight is pretty comical, not to mention embarrassing).

And then God, who I frequently doubt and question about whether or not He gives a lick about my meager little life, showed up in lights. As I sat in that courtroom with two others, we silently begged God to do what was best for this young man, but we let Him know what we really wanted was his freedom. We prayed that He fill this judge with mercy. And guess what? In spite of every single bit of evidence that made his lawyer's request sound like a long shot (he had already told us as much) and completely impractical, absurd, unlikely, and possibly even dangerous, she approved his release. I can't go into too much detail, but let's just say that an hour later, the young man had his picture taken outside, with the brilliant fall sunshine beaming down on his pale skin.

I have never witnessed a miracle this directly. I felt like God did some sort of Jedi-Mind-Trick on the courtroom that day. Ya know, like in *Star Wars* when the guards ask Obi-Wan for Luke and his companion's identification, he says, "You don't need to see their identification," and the guards respond, "We don't need to see their identification, move along!" That's how the Jedi-Mind-Trick works, and that's how crazy it was that this dear boy walked out of that courtroom to a new type of freedom. Made no sense at all; God's crazy like that.

And in the afterglow of experiencing this miracle, it only took me about two hours to swing back to the Dark Side over something of such little significance I won't even bother to bring it up.

In all this, I guess my point is that, as I have mentioned before, we are all broken and jacked-up and human, and this is most likely going to happen again and again and again. I am not proud of how easily I lose perspective and how demanding and childish and ungrateful I can be. But maybe God understands us better than we think. He knows I love Him madly, but occasionally behave badly. And He extends that same mercy to me that I witnessed Him extending through that judge. And He extends it to you too.

His mercies are new every morning…every day it's true, He makes all his mercies new.

Post-secret (or "What's your secret?")

I read a book in August, lying on the fake beach in downtown Chicago while my daughter and her friends went to Lollapalooza. This, for a 48-year-old female who has almost fully raised three children and survived cancer, packs all the fun and excitement I need to thoroughly enjoy myself. Of course, it was some heavy content--Stephen King's young adult book *Gwendy's Button Box*. I read all 164 widely spaced pages in two days (don't judge … I am a slow and simple reader). I have already talked about one of the book's major themes in my blog on "English as a second language" (found on my blog site: heathercarterwrites.com). I have been saving up the second one for a time that felt just right … now is that time, I guess.

Let me give you the sentence from the book that has been stuck in my mind since August:

> ***"Secrets are a problem, maybe the biggest problem of all. They weigh on the mind and take up space in the world."*** [70]

Gwendy has this thought as she becomes aware of the tremendous pressure she lives with after being given a box covered with buttons that hold power to control her immediate surroundings and even on the other side of the world. She has to keep it safe from others who might find it and use it for evil, as well as keep it safe from her own whims, fancies, or resentment fantasies. She has been given strict instructions by the giver not to let anyone know about the box. It becomes a veritable weight, a constant burden and distraction as she tries to go about her life, trying to look and act normal. She is ever mindful, even as she dates and succeeds in school and sports, of her box and its safety. She is always worrying someone might find it. She tells tales to her loved ones about where she is going so they won't know she is checking on the box. The secret consumes her every thought.

Take a moment, or several, to think of your "box," your biggest, scariest, and darkest secret.

Does it "weigh on your mind and take up space in the world"? It probably won't take you long to identify it, because it's just always right there. Even when you are fooling others, you are not fooling yourself. And it is slowly crushing you, robbing you of your freedom and your joy. Causing you to be imprisoned by your fear that someone might figure out your hiding spot. You can't let people too close because you wonder if you'll slip up or let yourself be vulnerable and give away its hiding place. You have imagined it over and over--the potential outcomes if this should happen: people might think you're an ogre, a hypocrite, a monster, a victim, someone unlovable, disgusting, irredeemable, unforgivable, unworthy. They might reject and shame you. These possibilities keep your resolve to hide it in strong force. You protect it at all costs. And that cost is pretty high.

What reignited my thoughts on this topic was an event my husband arranged for us to attend last month. I thought more people were aware of this New York Times bestseller than there actually are. When I told people we were going to the University of Illinois, Springfield to hear Frank Warren, the author of the *PostSecret* books, most had never heard of him or the book. We have had this book as a coffee table book for at least 10 years. And fun fact that I learned at the event: Frank Warren grew up in Springfield, Illinois (any of you Springfieldians know him?).

Here's the premise: in 2004 he passed out post cards to strangers with his home address on it, inviting them to share a secret. The only rules were that "it had to be true and it had to be something they had never shared with anyone before." It's also anonymous. After the first week he posted a few of them online and had 1,000 views. After week two he posted a few more and had 10,000 views. After week three, there were 100,000 views. The rest is history. Look it up. Today he has millions of postcards, filling an entire room, stacked almost to the ceiling.

I attended this event the night before I was to do one of my first "talks" to a local group of about 50 women. It reinforced that what I say and why I write is not only necessary for me, but for countless others who have often thought, "I am the only one."

The despair that comes from feeling like we are alone in our brokenness, our pain, our secrets, is crushing. It causes physical and mental illness, loneliness, and even death in our churches, our schools, and our town every single day. When we have secrets and keep them we slowly deteriorate.

In Recovery programs there is a saying, "We are only as sick as our secrets." You cannot work the 12 Steps successfully without passing through the steps that help you puke that junk out and let someone love you in spite of them. We have to reveal our secrets to God (which is redundant, since I believe He already knows), ourselves (which means we have to be alone with ourselves and reflect once in awhile), and to another person (the key to freedom and release).

Frank Warren continues to offer hope by giving people this same opportunity. During his talk, I wrote down several of his insights regarding secrets. One went something like this: *Secrets have stories; they can also offer truths. After seeing thousands of secrets,*

I understand that sometimes when we believe we are keeping a secret, that secret is actually keeping us.

At the end of the event I attended, he opened up two microphones and invited people to share their post-secret lives. There were lines curled around the corner and at one point he had to cut it off for the sake of time. People were brave and cried and hugged perfect strangers, and some, their best friend who they had kept this secret from. That is the reality of our world. Even though some of us have what we consider a "best friend," we are still in hiding and living in shame and fear, always trying to figure out the safest hiding place for our secret.

So, maybe today is the day of freedom for you. Or at least the beginning of it. Maybe you could start by sharing it anonymously with Frank. But eventually, I think sharing it with a person with skin on who can look you in the eye and tell you, "You're not alone and you are still worthy of love," will give you the most freedom. You have to be discerning about who that person is. Discretion is important, as well as the potential impact on the other person. Unloading the burden of your secret onto someone else that might be devastated by it, is not loving or wise. Pray about it. Seek counsel. Your goal must be for you to be free, but not at the expense of putting someone else into captivity.

I want to close this out by sharing a quote from *The Big Book of Alcoholics Anonymous*. I practically have it memorized, because I think it applies to anyone willing to expose the darkest places of their past in order to bring light and warmth to their present:

"We should be only too willing to bring former mistakes, no matter how grievous, out of their hiding places. Showing others who suffer how we were given help is the very thing which makes life seem worthwhile to us now. Cling to the thought that, in God's hands, the dark past is the greatest possession we have--the key to life and happiness for others. With it you can avert death and misery for them"[71] (and for ourselves, I might add).

(A portion of all *PostSecret* proceeds have been going to Suicide Prevention since the first of five books published in 2005. Don't let your secret bring you to such a place …)

Feelings aren't facts ...

Maybe not writing for a couple weeks has a direct correlation to the fact that I am struggling. Which came first? Who knows? What exactly am I struggling with? Well, ironically, during this Thanksgiving season--it's gratitude. At a time of year when even the most curmudgeonly people seem to pull out something to be grateful for, I am just not feeling it.

You have probably heard it said that "feelings aren't facts," but even when I make a gratitude list or encounter dear people I know I am thankful for, the *facts* remain and the *feelings* (read: warm, kind, sweet, tender) don't match.

I figured out that my attitude sort of stinks on this whole "thankfulness" topic while I was doing some reflective reading yesterday. The book has dated entries and this reading started with the same repetitious reminders that the author has addressed for the past seven days:

- "Be thankful in all circumstances."
- "Thankfulness takes the sting out of adversity."
- "Thank God frequently."
- "Thankfulness is a language of love."
- "Thanksgiving puts you in a proper relationship with God."
- "Fill your heart and mind with thankfulness."
- "When your mind is occupied with thankfulness, you have no time for worrying or complaining."[72]
- Blah, Blah, Blah. You get the idea. I was shocked at my response when I realized she was still stuck on this topic; a big eye roll. I mean, Thanksgiving is over, lady! Let's move on already!

I give you permission to pause it here and decide whether you want to continue reading what my bratty-sounding self has to say (maybe ever again!) …

For those of you who are still with me--I just have to say that I am not proud of this posture and it makes me feel like I have no right to write anything at all until I get my junk together. But I have learned a couple of things from writing a few hundred blogs. One, when I stop writing regularly, bad things happen in my soul (since the majority of what I write helps me first and you second--I can't give away what I don't possess). And two, when I share the stuff I am most ashamed to share, that's when people seem to connect the most. I suppose I understand. I feel weird and isolated and crazy most of the time, and I don't always find hope when I hear motivating talk from someone whose life seems spotless and never appears to struggle with "temporary insanity"--being tempted to live counter to what they know to be true in their heart. I just don't relate, and despair and self-pity take over.

So, what am I gonna do about my lack of "happy" feelings and my pessimistic, prickly emotions?

Well, as I have said, awareness is the first step in making some changes. Now that I am aware, I can make some phone calls and dialogue with people and God. And I can know that "this too shall pass," because sometimes we just get in a funk for no apparent reason and we don't have to flog ourselves over it.

Don't worry about me. I'll do what I need to do to get "better." But even though I started this blog to confess my grouchy, juvenile attitude and maybe give some insight into how to "fix" it, I think that God has other intentions for it. What I hope you hear is that "you're not alone." I am still here for you, still as messed up as ever, and I will walk next to you as we "trudge this happy road to destiny" together. Never, ever forget that.

When is enough enough?

My yoga meditation for today was, "Today I am ENOUGH, and I trust you with my future." Mine are always some sort of reminder to "get God in there" as I start my day. This one is particularly powerful for me at Christmastime, a time when I feel sub-par in multiple areas. Maybe you have been feeling it too.

I have caught myself worrying that I don't have ***enough*** money to buy this or ***enough*** to pay for that (now that I just swiped my credit card). I am certain I don't have ***enough*** hours in my day to finish my shopping and get everything wrapped in the next six days. I feel like I am not a good ***enough*** friend or neighbor because I haven't baked one cookie or Christmas-y treat for them, or for my own family, for that matter. I haven't celebrated ***enough*** with people I care about; I haven't spent enough time sitting quietly in my living room enjoying my Christmas tree and I haven't done enough holiday activities or engaged in ***enough*** of our usual Christmas traditions. I haven't reflected ***enough*** on the real reason for the season. My home doesn't look ***enough*** like a Martha Stewart catalogue. I haven't sent ***enough*** Christmas cards out (OK, so zero Christmas cards is legitimately "not enough") and I am scared to death that I'll realize on Christmas Eve that I don't have ***enough*** presents for one of my kids (because we all know everything has to be even). Oh, and did I mention that lately I haven't gotten ***enough*** sleep or eaten ***enough*** fruits and vegetables or worked out ***enough***? Sigh …

You might say that I need to relax and lighten up. Take it easy on myself, for Pete's sake. You might be right.

But isn't this the battle we all feel drawn to engage in during this single month of the year? We feel like the answer to the question, "When is enough *enough*?" is "never" when it comes to the scramble of the holidays.

One of the reasons I do not feel "enough" is because I compare myself with others and determine I don't measure up. The other is because my expectations are unreasonable, unrealistic, and unattainable. When I focus on trying to meet such expectations, I feel less than. Like a failure. Like not ***enough***.

Today (and I will try not to wish I had practiced this meditation soon ***enough*** to enjoy this season more fully) I will remind myself again and again and again that who I am and what I have done is ***enough***. It's enough for me and enough for others and most certainly enough for God.

Underlinable

I have been reading a book that was loaned to me by a friend.

Loaned. Not given.

As a general rule, when given a book on loan, one should protect that book, keeping the pages smooth (no dog-earing the corners) and barely opening it so as not to crack the spine. One should avoid using the book to set one's coffee cup on so it won't spill on the couch. One should also refrain, no matter how poignant a word, sentence, or phrase of said book, from underlining or highlighting anything.

Unless one just can't refrain one page longer and wildly lets her pen fly.

I made it all the way to page 73.

That's when I couldn't take it anymore and began to underline insights that I needed to hear and wanted to revisit in the future.

I don't read much that isn't non-fiction/self-help/inspirational because I actually hate reading.

My brain considers reading work, not something you do for enjoyment.

I have a pretty short attention span which is why I only read about a chapter at a time (or less, if the chapter is really long!) before I can't focus anymore.

I also seem to forget what I read … unless I underline it.

It helps me really "hear" what is being said through the text.

Sometimes I get a little crazy and try to listen to an audio book. That's sort of a disaster. I end up only understanding about half of the book because A, my mind wanders off and B, I can't underline anything.

This morning, as I finished up this book, I decided to go back to the beginning and re-read the first 72 pages and underline anything that I didn't learn the first time when I was reading "pen-free." There was some pretty good stuff in there!

That's when I had this thought about how my life can be divided up into days that have moments or conversations or insights that are underlined and days that are just a run-on of activities and actions that are void and without intention and laden with duty.

Next to my sitting spot on my couch I have a basket of about 20 books that I have already read, at least once. Many of them I re-read every year and am delighted when I see that something I underlined the year before has actually been a growth area for me.

Other times I am surprised to pull a nugget of truth off a page that was just plain naked. How could I have missed this last time I read it?!

By now, I have learned that I just wasn't ready to receive that truth yet, or I was a different person or at a different place in my life then; I didn't need to hear it until now. I couldn't.

I want my life to be marked up—underlined (maybe, if I get a little wild, even highlighted or starred or circled!). I don't want to go through several "pages" of my story where there is nothing worth underlining.

When I start to read a book that doesn't compel me to underline anything, it goes back on the shelf or to Goodwill. I have no interest in finishing it.

Living a life worth underlining doesn't mean constant adventure or entertainment or morose, reflective thinking. For me, I think it means I look for ways to do the regular stuff with intentionality and awareness that there is something bigger going on than what is right in front of me.

It means that I look around for someone to serve and listen for God's promptings to engage in my life in a way that has purpose outside of my tasks and chores and obligations.

Each day I am writing more of the story of my life. If I re-read it, would I come across anything that would make not underlining it unbearable?

Lord, help me live a life that is underlinable.

Endnotes

1. Sarah Young, *Jesus Calling* (Nashville TN: Thomas Nelson, 2004), 137.
2. On the album All the People Said Amen, Essential Records, 2013.
3. Oswald Chambers, *My Utmost for His Highest* (Westwood NJ: Barbour and Company, Inc., 1963),118.
4. brainyquote.com, accessed May 11, 2016.
5. *How Al-Anon Works* (Chicago: Anon Press, 1995), 82.
6. Ibid., 82.
7. Chambers, 187.
8. *The Alcoholics Anonymous Big Book*, 4th edition, (Chicago: Anon Press, 2001), 60.
9. Ibid., 76.
10. Ibid., 59.
11. Ibid., 59.
12. Chambers, 304.
13. L.B. Cowman, *Streams in the Desert* (Grand Rapids MI: Zondervan, 1997), 421.
14. Ibid., 421.
15. *How Al-Anon Works* (Chicago: Anon Press, 1995), 50,51.
16. Steven Furtick, *Crash the Chatterbox* (Colorado Springs CO: Multnomah, 2015).
17. *Courage to Change: One Day at a Time in Al-Anon II* (Virginia Beach, VA: Al-Anon Family Group Headquarters, 1992), 56.
18. Chambers, 286.
19. Ibid., 286.
20. Young, 305.
21. Ibid., 305.

22. Ibid., 331.
23. kaywarren.com, accessed December 5, 2016.
24. *Courage to Change, 340.*
25. Ibid., 340.
26. Glennon Doyle, *Love Warrior* (New York NY: Flat Iron, 2017), 113.
27. quotationspage.com, accessed February 1, 2017.
28. Young, 9.
29. Richmond W., *Twenty-Four Hours a Day* (Center City MN: Hazelden Foundation, 2013 reprint edition).
30. *The Light Between Oceans.* Derek Cianfrance. Los Angeles.Touchstone Pictures, 2016.
31. *Courage to Change,* 289.
32. Chambers, 168.
33. *National Lampoon's Christmas Vacation.* Jeremiah S. Chechik, Los Angeles. Hughes Entertainment, 1989.
34. Chambers,154.
35. Ibid., 154.
36. Ibid., 154.
37. *The AA Big Book*, 59.
38. Richard Rohr, *Breathing Under Water* (Cincinnati OH: Franciscan Media, 2011),
39. "Magnificent." No Line on the Horizon, Mercury; Island; Interscope, 2009.
40. Ibid.
41. tonycampolo.org, accessed March 2, 2017.
42. *Courage to Change*, 249.
43. Richard Rohr, *Immortal Diamond* (Hoboken NJ: Jossey-Bass, 2013), 19.
44. Tom Petty. Hard Promises, Backstreet Records, 1981.
45. The Byrds. "Turn! Turn! Turn!" Columbia Records, 1965.
46. L.B. Cowman, *Streams in the Desert* (Grand Rapids MI: Zondervan, 1997)
47. John Francis Xavier O'Conor, *A Study of Francis Thompson's Hound of Heaven* (London: John Lane Co., 1912).

48. Young, 9.
49. "Garments of Praise." Revival in Belfast, Integrity Music, 1999.
50. Reinhold Niebuhr, *The Essential Reinhold Niebuhr: Selected Essays and Addresses.* (New Haven: Yale University Press, 1987), 251.
51. Jordan Gaines Lewis, "Smells Ring Bells," *Psychology Today*, Vol. #, January 12, 2015.
52. Young, 31.
53. *The AA Big Book*, 59.
54. annerobertson.org, accessed March 14, 2018.
55. Brenè Brown, *The Gifts of Imperfection* (Center City, MN: Hazelden Publishing, 2010), 80.
56. Marianne Williamson, *A Return to Love* (New York: Harper Collins, 1993).
57. Rohr, *Breathing Underwater.*
58. Ibid.
59. *The AA Big Book*, 59.
60. Brown, 108.
61. *The AA Big Book*, 59.
62. Chambers, 198.
63. *Bill Cosby: Himself* (Jemmin, Inc., 1983).
64. *How Al Anon Works*, 78.
65. Young, 273.
66. Richard Rohr, *Falling Upward* (Hoboken NJ: Jossey-Bass, 2011), xiv.
67. Ibid., xv.
68. *Courage to Change*, 283.
69. Chambers, 283.
70. Richard Chizmar and Stephen King, *Gwendy's Button Box* (New York: Gallery Books, 2017), 30.
71. *The AA Big Book*, 124.
72. *Young, 340-345.*
73. Zach Williams. "Fear, He is a Liar." Chain Breaker, Essential Music, 2016.

74. *Courage to Change*, 15.
75. *How Al-Anon Works,* 45,46.
76. Williamson, 5.
77. Ibid., 6.
78. Ibid., 22.
79. Ibid., 22.
80. Rohr, *Immortal Diamond*, 15.
81. Williamson, 6.
82. Ibid., 7.
83. drleaf.com, accessed July 16, 2019.
84. Chambers, 273.
85. Young, 345.
86. Chambers, 4.
87. Young, 7.
88. *Courage to Change*, 65.
89. Brenè Brown, *The Power of Vulnerability* (Sounds True, Inc., 2012).
90. *Courage to Change*, 44.
91. Ibid, 33.

Acknowledgments

Thank you to my husband, children, parents and in-laws who have encouraged me to publish and who have been the subject of many a blog. They have all been good sports about their lives being laid bare before the world so that we can bring redemption out of the hard stuff.

A huge thank you to all my friends for putting up with me and loving me no matter what. I am fully aware I am high maintenance, and I am grateful that they love me in spite of my craziness!

Thank you to my friend Lucy Dalton-Lackie who did the arduous work of sorting through my endnotes. That's true friendship right there!

Thank you to June Agamah for writing her own story and connecting me to Joni Sullivan (Buoyancy Public Relations) who ultimately connected me to Shane Crabtree (Christian Book Services) who was willing to help me make this book a reality.

A huge shout out to Rachel Eastvold for being my Social Media Manager. I would have given up a long time ago if I had had to write my blogs and figure out how to post it creatively. She keeps me from looking antiquated and getting buried in the social media world that confounds me!

And it goes without saying that above all, I am grateful to a gracious God who gives a gift to someone like me to share with someone like you. I am humbled beyond words that I am still alive to say anything at all, and that He has given me the opportunity to say anything that matters. He indeed gives beauty for ashes.

Praise be to our merciful Father and
the source of all comfort, who comforts us
in all our troubles so that we can comfort others.
When they are troubled, we will be able to
give them the same comfort God has given us.
***2 Corinthians 1:3,4 (NLT)**

To read previous and new posts,
please go to heathercarterwrites.com.

Remember to sign up to have any new
blogs emailed to you directly!

How to host a Soul-Selfie Book Club

Suggested Format (but feel free to work with whatever your group wants. And let me know how it goes!)

*Decide on length of study (how many weeks) and divide up the book accordingly.

*Each person should come with a copy of the book.

*During the first week, read the section on "Why I write" from beginning of the book and review "Ground Rules" (see below).

*Contact me through email (heathercartersoul-selfie@gmail.com) or my website and arrange for me to be at your first meeting to tell my story and kick it off (in person, Zoom, FaceTime, whatever works!)

*Encourage people to come prepared to read and discuss one or two entries at each week's gathering.

*Begin by agreeing on the first entry. One person starts and reads a few paragraphs and then next person in the circle reads and so on and so forth until it's complete.

*At that point whoever wants to go first shares their reaction (use questions below if you need help) for 3 or 4 minutes. Everyone listens and lets them talk without interrupting or giving advice. From there, the turn passes to each person in the circle in order. Just pass the Kleenex box when your turn is over. (If someone doesn't care to share, they can pass and just listen. But I have found that many are willing to share if it is simply their turn to do so).

*After everyone has a chance to share, read the next blog (which can be decided on based on what people have read the week before).

Ground Rules:

*Remind people that what is said in the room stays in the room. Confidentiality is paramount. No cross-talking/interrupting.

*Don't think you have to "lead." Everyone should take ownership. You are just the facilitator. So no excuses.

*It's not about fixing or giving advice. Keep the focus on you, your experience and your understanding of God.

*Limit verbal affirmations during each person's "share." Let them talk uninterrupted.

*Suggestion only: Pass a Kleenex box as you indicate whose turn it is. Let them cry if they need to. Let them use Kleenex if they need to or let the tears flow!

*Try to keep each sub-group fairly small. If you get 10 or more split into two groups so everyone has time to read and share.

*Show up even if you didn't do your reading. No shaming. You and others might need you to be there!

*Respect: remember everyone is on their own journey. We are all exactly where we are supposed to be. Go easy on yourself and especially on others. Be tolerant. Gracious. Accepting. Don't assume you know what they believe about faith, God, life, etc. Only speak for yourself and consider how you say it.

*Be yourself and don't compare.

As you read, use the following questions to help you share when it is your turn:

1. How have I experienced/thought/felt something similar in my life?
2. If it is past tense, how has my attitude/belief/thinking changed as a result?

3. If it is a present situation or thought/belief pattern, what can the group do to help you find perspective/hope/healing or celebration in it?

Feedback from those who have been part of Soul-Selfie Book Clubs:

Absolutely loved reading *Soul-Selfie*. Being in a book club with the author & others made the book so real & enabled me to do some soul searching & healing. It was comforting knowing that so many others share in the same struggles, despite the situation being completely different.

-Ravita

Through Heather's book club we learned to take responsibility for our own stuff and listen to each person. It created a non-threatening environment, so people can find their own way to Truth. All that helped me see that our group could find that safe place and being prompted by your blogs, to study and have the same focus by just sharing our experiences. Acceptance and tolerance. No judgement.

-Grace